BLACK FEMINISM IN QUALITATIVE INQUIRY

Recently, Black women have taken the world stage in national politics, popular culture, professional sports, and bringing attention to racial injustice in policing and the judicial system. However, rarely are Black women acknowledged and highlighted for their efforts to understand the social problems confronting our generation and those generations that came before us. In the post-civil rights era, research faculty and theoreticians must acknowledge the marginalization of Black women scholars' voices in contemporary qualitative scholarship and debates.

Black Feminism in Qualitative Inquiry: A Mosaic for Writing Our Daughter's Body engages qualitative inquiry to center the issues and concerns of Black women as researcher(s) and the researched while simultaneously questioning the ostensible innocence of qualitative inquiry, including methods of data collection, processes of data analysis, and representations of human experiences and identities. The text centers "daughtering" as the onto-epistemological tool for approaches to Black feminist and critical race data analysis in qualitative inquiry.

Advanced and novice researchers interested in decolonizing methodologies and liberatory tools of analysis will find the text useful for cultural, education, political, and racial critiques that center the intersectional identities and interpretations of Black women and girls and other people of color. Daughtering as a tool of analysis in Black feminist qualitative inquiry is our own cultural and spiritual way of being, doing, and performing decolonizing work.

Venus E. Evans-Winters is an Associate Professor of Education in the Department of Educational Administration and Foundations at Illinois State University. She is also faculty affiliate with Women and Gender Studies, African American Studies, and Ethnic Studies. Her research interests are educational policy, qualitative inquiry, and critical race feminism in education.

FUTURES OF DATA ANALYSIS IN QUALITATIVE RESEARCH

Series Editor: Kakali Bhattacharya

Kansas State University

The books in the series *Futures of Data Analysis in Qualitative Research* document the various ways in which qualitative researchers approach data analysis within the context of qualitative inquiry. The series specifically encourages work done from various intersected margins which focus on ways in which a researcher might have had to break rank with traditions, established practices, or privileged, dominant approaches. The books consider multiple aspects including, but not limited to, role of theory, ethics, positionality, processes and their role in generating insights.

While the emphasis of the series is analysis, books in the series could also subvert how analysis is understood and practiced in qualitative inquiry if established discourses are incommensurable for their specific inquiries. Focusing on non-traditional or reconfiguration of the familiar in analysis, the series encourages books written from various interpretive, critical, deconstructive, or other contemporary orientations. The books not only offer narrative details of qualitative data analysis process with examples, but also new ontoepistemic, theoretical, methodological, and substantive knowledge.

For more information about the series or to submit a book proposal, please contact Series Editor Kakali Bhattacharya, kakalibh@ksu.edu.

Volumes in this series include:

Black Feminism in Qualitative Inquiry
A Mosaic for Writing Our Daughter's Body
Venus E. Evans-Winters

For a full list of titles in this series, please visit:
www.routledge.com/series/FDAQR

BLACK FEMINISM IN QUALITATIVE INQUIRY

A Mosaic for Writing Our Daughter's Body

Venus E. Evans-Winters

Routledge
Taylor & Francis Group

LONDON AND NEW YORK

First published 2019
by Routledge
2 Park Square, Milton Park, Abingdon, Oxon OX14 4RN

and by Routledge
52 Vanderbilt Avenue, New York, NY 10017

Routledge is an imprint of the Taylor & Francis Group, an informa business

British Library Cataloguing in Publication Data
A catalogue record for this book is available from the British Library

Library of Congress Cataloging-in-Publication Data
Names: Evans-Winters, Venus E., author.
Title: Black feminism in qualitative inquiry : a mosaic for writing our
daughter's body / Venus E. Evans-Winters.
Description: Abingdon, Oxon ; New York, NY : Routledge, 2018. |
Series: Futures of data analysis in qualitative research |
Includes bibliographical references and index.
Identifiers: LCCN 2018044573| ISBN 9781138486218 (hardback : alk. paper) |
ISBN 9781138486225 (pbk. : alk. paper) |
ISBN 9781351046077 (ebook : alk. paper)
Subjects: LCSH: Feminism--Research--United States. |
Black women--United States. | African American women. |
African American feminists. | Racism--United States. | Qualitative research.
Classification: LCC HQ1181.U5 E93 2018 | DDC 305.48/896073--dc23
LC record available at https://lccn.loc.gov/2018044573

ISBN: 978-1-138-48621-8 (hbk)
ISBN: 978-1-138-48622-5 (pbk)
ISBN: 978-1-351-04607-7 (ebk)

Typeset in Bembo
by Taylor & Francis Books

To my grandmother and mama.
Sister.
African man child (Stephen) and Princess (Serena).
Every student who has called me Dr. V.
To every Black daughter—daughtering.

CONTENTS

ACKNOWLEDGMENTS

For many authors, like myself, the acknowledgment section of the book is the most difficult part to write. My support system extends across various communities, contexts, social groups, and personalities. My expressions of gratitude span across time and space beginning with my grandmother's house to the corn fields of Champaign–Urbana to my current faculty position at Illinois State University. Because I cannot thank all of those who have shaped me and ideas presented in this book, I will attempt to name those most present for me as the book was birthed. First, I would like to thank my family—the Evans clan and Winters. I, especially, want to thank my two children who were put on the back burner while I completed this book project. There were many times that I dazed out into space or I stayed in my pajamas all day, sitting in my favorite chair, and clicked away at my laptop while pretending to be present. As the novelist Toni Morrison admitted, when you are a writer, it is the children who sacrifice their mother. I am a full-time university professor and part-time writer, and therefore, my children certainly sacrificed as my mind and body danced between them, teaching, and writing this book. I thank my African man child and princess. Second, I want to thank my grandmother and mother whose spirits I relied upon to "take me back." It was their spirit energy that I called upon to help me process, contemplate, and heal from memories and stories. Next, I express much gratitude to the boldly creative Dr. Kakali (Queen B) Bhattacharya who became my biggest supporter and cheerleader when I complained to her about the standardization of qualitative thinking and writing. I explained to her that I could not continue to participate any longer in the ghettoization and colonization of Black women's intellectual labor. This book, ironically enough, is the result of our conversations and sister-girl talk healing sessions. I would also like to thank every other woman scholar of color who supports, advocates, and fights for other women of color scholars unapologetically. Further, I am particularly grateful for every sister, fictive or kin, whose story is (re)told in this book; every girl I have played with on the block, every girl research participant, and every high school girl or college student I have mentored. Finally, I owe much gratitude to the team at Routledge, Hannah and Matthew, for keeping me organized and on track for the completion of this book. You all prove that the decolonization of knowledge is a team effort.

INTRODUCTION

In *Black Feminism in Qualitative Inquiry: A Mosaic for Writing Our Daughter's Body*, I catechize qualitative inquiry from a critical race analysis and Black feminist/womanist interpretation of the social world. On the one hand, I admittedly enjoy reading traditional academic qualitative texts that attempt to define qualitative concepts, paradigmatic traditions, and shifts, and quixotically explain methodologies. On the other hand, I find a sense of *pleasure* in reading non-traditional qualitative texts that inscribe the written word to introduce audiences to a research study, research participants involved in the study, and the social context of the study. I am emphatically stimulated, intellectually and aesthetically, by qualitative presentations that use the written word to mentally place the reader in the physical environment where the study took place, and sophisticatedly breathe life into research participants' personal histories and commentary in ways that emotionally connect the reader to the research subject at hand.

Despite my love for the skill, talent, and giftedness of qualitative researchers who bring pleasurable experiences to the reader, research faculty and theoreticians must acknowledge the marginalization of Black women scholars' voices in contemporary qualitative scholarship and debates. Although Black women have always conducted research using qualitative methodologies, rarely are Black women given space to *play with* or theorize methodological moves in qualitative inquiry. For this book, I engage qualitative inquiry to center the issues and concerns of Black women as researcher(s) and the researched while simultaneously questioning the ostensible innocence of qualitative inquiry, including methods of data collection, processes of data analysis, and representations of human experiences and identities.

While many qualitative research scholars from diverse racial, ethnic, gender, linguistic, religious, and cultural backgrounds claim to be inveterate reflective observers of the social world and critics of research traditions in general, many of us who find comfort in the qualitative tradition fail to particularize the research experience and continue to reproduce linear, formulaic, static conversations on the analysis of qualitative research. In the midst of disciplinary conversations that question the purpose of research, research findings, and the research process itself, it is essential that such conversations include diverse perspectives and representations of qualitative work.

In this book, I blur the boundaries between research, theory, and practice, and I intentionally explore, interrupt, unveil, and instigate the confusion, or the lack thereof, of the naming, doing, and writing up of the present qualitative moment while centering my experiences as a Black woman scholar interested in the lived experiences of Black girls and women. When I imagine a book that focuses on how data (and all that it has claimed to be and represent) comes to be understood, I imagine a book that I would want to read; and a book that I can empathize with the *characters* (I will explain more about the use of this term and discursive move in the book), scenes, languages and conversations, emotions, events, and research quandaries relevant at that moment. More poignantly, I yearn for a qualitative volume that is reflective of my own personal experiences or the experiences of those around me, or those whom I have come in contact with at some point in my life journey.

Moreover, this is an opportune time to present alternative perspectives on qualitative research as a process and product. For example, a common platitude in qualitative research is that our worldviews color how we interpret data or what we see, hear, touch, smell, and taste. However, I extend the conversation by asseverating that Black women's ways of knowing, cultural and spiritual beliefs continue to be marginalized, suppressed, or bastardized and propagated as trite or esoteric at best. Sadly, conversations on data analysis in qualitative circles are still dominated and policed by those of the White educated elite. Consequently, data analysis and products that come forth out of qualitative inquiry are more reflective of White middle class culture, or a limited worldview, than representative of the richness and dynamicism of those of us who live and exist on the margins of society. There is a need for research texts grounded in hybrid languages, cultures, thought processes, and discursive dances.

Fieldnotes

I adopt narrative, prose poetry, and performance to construct this book or *presentations of data*. The human experience is dynamic, and so should be our analyses in telling/writing tales of it. It would become more than obvious that I am not married to any one qualitative tradition or methods of analysis; and skeptical of any formulaic and categorizations of the documentation of lived experience. Fieldnote 1 titled "A mosaic of Black feminism" provides a brief overview of Black feminism as I imagine it in qualitative inquiry with all of the messiness and possibility.

At a time when many intellectual activists are re-imagining and re-examining our intellectual roots, I too am treading upon a rebellious phase where I ask, "Is this analytical tool working for me or not? Does Black feminism work for the young Black women who I have come to represent at home and in higher education classrooms?" All critical theory is open for criticism, even our beloved Black feminism/womanism. I open the fieldnote with an adolescent reflection of how I was making judgment calls on my grandmother's actions, but soon realized that my grandmother was performing identities to navigate her social environment. I adapted my grandmother's "style" or habit of mind to contemplate the role of Black feminism in my approaches to qualitative inquiry.

Fieldnote 1, like every fieldnote in this book, offers a mosaic of Black feminism in qualitative inquiry. Next in fieldnote 2, I introduce a prose poem to demonstrate how one comes to understand her *place* or positionality within a community and the social world. Our place in the world shapes how we consume and produce knowledge as well as how we choose to disseminate knowledge. In our moments of *playing with* data, or stated differently, in conscience engagement in the interpretation of data, we draw upon formal academic training in research methods, but we also consciously and subconsciously rely on cultural intuition and prior childhood and adult socialization within our primary culture(s).

In this second fieldnote, I imply that many culturally and linguistically diverse scholars at times actually draw upon formal academic training counter intuitively. In our excitement to engage in the research process and learn all that we were taught in our graduate studies, at times, methods and (ethical) choices made in the research process feel foreign and inauthentic. Other times, such intellectual maneuvers feel abusive or exploitative; yet, many move forward in the process in order to meet the necessary class and program requirements for matriculation toward an advance degree. For the record, it is not always that these research protocols are unsophisticated or abusive, but from the standpoint of Black women and other women of color, they present as culturally perverse. Surely we bring our own cultural baggage to the research process.

Fieldnote 2 raises the following important questions as it relates to qualitative inquiry and so-called data analysis: How does early socialization, culture, identity, and *place* shape how one produces, consumes, and disseminate knowledge? How do we conscientiously bring forth our ways of knowing, and *performing* knowing, into the research process? How might our knowledge performances inform data analysis? How does culturally informed interpretations of pleasure and pain, the public and private, discipline and punishment inform researchers' and participants' understanding of the benefits and risks involved in the research process? In other words, how do covenants with our culture(s) of origin inform research ethics and protocols, what gets told (and does not get told) in the analysis process, and how is data represented?

In fieldnote 3, I discuss intellectual servitude or how higher education socializes all students to serve the agenda of the White middle class. One of the biggest myths feeding the psyches of educators is that young Black people enter classrooms and the learning process as blank slates. In the U.S., we are socialized to perceive Black people as morally, intellectually, physically, culturally, and aesthetically inferior to White people. Media, religion, schooling, parental upbring, peer relationships, etc., teach White people that Black people are naturally inferior and that White people are rightfully superior. Consequently, the average teacher views Black students as inherently "deficient," lacking of purpose, and in need of mending. Informed by so-called objective science, education systems perpetuate racialized myths of inherited deficiency. To decolonize research methodologies, we first must work on decolonizing the mind.

Fieldnote 4, "Telling stories: Black girls' thumbprints," highlights a childhood memory that exposes how the intersection of race, class, and gender shapes Black women's *relationship with* knowledge. I unapologetically demonstrate and contend that research and writing practices by Black women should be witnessed as subtle acts of disobedience and defiance against race and gender (and age) oppression. The question for scholars (and active readers) is how do we evaluate the authenticity of Black women's stories and truth claims, especially considering the diversity in Black girls' and women's experiences, based on age, geographical location, socioeconomic status, sexuality, birth order, religion, family structure, physical aesthetics, language, physical and intellectual abilities, etc.? Dis/obedience may be a determining aspect or "mosaic" of authenticity and criticality in womanist (Afro-centric and woman-centered) data analysis and *thumbprint* representations.

In "(De)commodification of the Black girl narrative," fieldnote 5, I open with a presentation of a pedagogical reflection as an artifact, titled *Why I need Black feminism*. The reflection is an example of blurring the boundaries between theory and performance. The reflection derives after an experience teaching a Black feminism class with a lecture hall full of mostly young Black women and other women of color. Daily the students looked visibly confused about my need for Black feminism, and wondered throughout the semester how this theory could relate to their personal lives back at home. They also wondered why my visible middle-class status alongside an apparent pro-Black stance needed Black feminism as a political tool.

In the subsequent narrative following *Why I need Black feminism*, I share a story of my grappling with the commodification of Black girls' narratives. In the narrative, I directly address the question of who is permitted to become an authority on Black girls' and women's experiences. The purpose of fieldnote 5 is to demonstrate the blurring of theory, performance, and critique in qualitative inquiry. Together, the pedagogical reflection (as artifact) and the narrative (as story) demonstrate that the analysis and presentation of qualitative data is informed by the researcher's worldview, lived experiences, and identities. Asserted throughout the fieldnote is that through a critical race and gendered lens, our qualitative presentations and performances can shift from pathology to agency, resilience, and showcasing acts of resistance. The fieldnote addresses the questions "How do qualitative researchers help make the concerns of Black women the concerns of research? And how might qualitative researchers make the concerns of research the concerns of Black women?" I intentionally in the data analysis process expose the researcher's vulnerability, resilience, and agency alongside participants' (and other social actors who influence the researcher's interpretations and ponderings) vulnerability, resilience, and agency.

In fieldnote 6, "Voice in re/presentation," I present a multilayered ethnographic text. In the continual methodological choice to provide a mosaic of Black women's voice and experience, I showcase various forms of data re/presentations. In this particular section, the audience views the research and participant as the knower and an authority on Black women's experiences. One witnesses first hand that I draw from multiple sources in the data analysis process, including my own ethnographic gaze (self-observation), personal narrative and journal notes, participant her-story, secondary sources, interview transcripts, etc.

Moreover, I suggest that data analysis can be a co-constructed piece of artwork. In particular, the fieldnote, text (or chapter) itself is my stage. At some moments, I am the main character, and at other moments, the "data" is the main storyline, while at other times, Nanette (the research participant) is center stage. My point in playing *with* text, or the re/presentation of text as voice, here is to demonstrate the significance of researcher **and** participant agency, voice, and authority. Africana womanist methodology qualitative inquiry acknowledges the importance of balance, reciprocity, and the authority of the Black woman's researcher's voice and the Black woman participant's voice. This fieldnote is a mosaic; or in African American vernacular, I am straight freestyling, playing double-dutch, and hitting the cypher. If I had to de-cypher/decipher this fieldnote, I would state that it is an attempt at inscribing a multiple consciousness grounded in an African womanist/ Black feminist onto-epistemology and search for synchronicity in our research performances. Evident is a self-consciousness, collective (un)consciousness, and a moral call to action as a part of the analysis process itself.

Accordingly, I conclude the fieldnote (six) with a demonstration of the research technique I call *politicking*. *Politicking* reminds us of the purposes of data analysis, which is not simply to pleasure the researcher's or onlookers' (readers) sensibilities. Here centering a Black/African-centered/womanist ontoepistomology, I use the research relationship and process itself as an opportunity to bring awareness to the socio-political conditions our research participants' encounter in their daily contexts and any other personal or social factors we believe should be informed by or highlighted in the research presentation.

"Writing my daughter's body," fieldnote 7, is an ethnographic narrative that reveals my conscious and subconscious ponderings in the field. Unveiled reflections on academic training, culture and socialization, and mothering raise questions about how the ethics of qualitative inquiry are posed. In *episodes*, I attempt to articulate my internal struggle with research *on*—as opposed to with—young people. An episode is an incident in the course of a series of events, in a person's life or experience, or an incident or scene within a narrative. From a psychology perspective, an episode may also represent a distinctive period in an individual's life that includes a heightened (psychosomatic) mood, usually abnormal (e.g. depressive, irritation, fear, anger, etc.).

Throughout the discussion in fieldnote 7, we witness my various internal selves in a conversation, regarding my daughter's presence in my service work with West African girls representing various ethnic/tribal affiliations. The voice of my *academic self* represents my formal training as a scholar, researcher, and pedagogue. Whereas *cultural reflections* are representative of the cultural understandings that one brings to her ethnographic contexts and pedagogical endeavors. Cultural reflections here represent my internalized beliefs, morals, and values that I borrow from my primary culture(s). Most qualitative researchers are taught to be cognizant of their own cultures and how this influences the research process. Lastly, I engage in *mother speak*. Mother speak represents for me an intuition—or internal voice—derived from socialization (to play my role as a girl, woman, and child), formal learning (e.g. reading books, stories, and other texts on parenting and child development), and biological instinct. At any moment in the field, these multiples selves, multiple voices are sometimes in conflict while at other times congruent.

Fieldnote 8, "Unveiling the mask," presents shared artifacts (i.e. pieces of data) given to me by a research participant. These data become part of a larger narrative of Black women's ways of coping, agency, resilience, and resistance. In this field-note, Black women's poetry and multiple ways of knowing and expressing emotions are showcased. What is the mask? Why do we wear the mask? How is the mask unveiled in the research process? How does the research process itself become a mask? When does the researcher decide to peel back the mask in data analysis? The intent of this fieldnote is to unveil Black women's *collective unconscious* as it reveals itself in qualitative inquiry.

Next, in fieldnote 9, "An inconvenient truth," I respond to the question "How do we bring our research to life in a way that audiences can feel what we feel as we walk this world as young/Black/woman/researcher/participant?" To begin to answer this question, I explain how I turned to data analysis techniques that were reflective of youth culture and Black girlhood when researching with young women of color. The fieldnote opens with my introduction to the youth researchers and our engagement in youth participatory action research. Then, the conversation explains the purpose of the youth research study and what they revealed about the girls' schooling in high density urban schools. Subsequently, I paint a portrait of how inconvenient truths come to fruition in the data analysis process. Audiences will have the opportunity to contemplate the utility of multiple forms of representation beyond printed text that privileges adult literacy and the written tradition. Youth artwork centered on theme of harsh discipline policies will be displayed.

In "Text messages: a call and response," the title of fieldnote 10, I showcase raw text messages as data. The text messages presented expand over the course of two years. In an analysis of the data, I make the case for reciprocity in qualitative inquiry. It will be more than obvious to readers that I draw upon my background as a qualitative researcher and social worker to build the relationship between myself and my hesitant "informant." My informant in this case was reluctant to get to know me beyond the classroom, because she thought that she would end up in one of my books.

However, as she got to know me as a person, she became curious of who I was as a scientist. In fact, she believed that I relied too heavily and trusted science too much instead of religion, in particular Christianity. In conversation, it became obvious that she thought my beliefs in science/rationality would rub off on her, and I feared her religious/irrational ideas would rub off on me. Text messaging, I believe, became a safe entry point for both of us into each other's world. Fortunately, for me, Skyye, my text message informant wanted to make it into one of my books, or become a "case study" as she put it.

Interestingly enough, "Text messages" also exposes my psyche beyond the researcher role, because the so-called informant began to boldly (but respectively in the Black tradition) ask me questions and interpret my behavior and words in her messages. While taking advantage of text messages and other images (i.e. journal entries), I also purposefully exhibit reciprocity and vulnerability in the research process. The ultimate intent is to show how data analysis can also be *soul work* that serves to heal thyself and (un)willing participants.

Finally, in fieldnote 11, I conclude the book with a response to calls for de/colonizing methodologies in qualitative pursuits. I provide a brief overview of descriptions of de/colonization methodologies, and put forth the case that the body of work presented in this book begins to open up the conversation of the place of Africana methodologies in qualitative inquiry, data analysis, and performance.

Playing with data in the dark

We have more women of color, especially women of African ancestry, than ever before entering higher education institutions as undergraduate and graduate students and faculty. Recent demographic trends will undoubtedly influence how we develop curriculum and pedagogy in colleges and universities, including in our research courses. Like all students, these women will want to see themselves in research texts, and be able to access and conduct research that meets their academic and personal needs.

Secondly, institutions are experiencing these demographic and cultural shifts in education, at a time when current political conditions threaten to suffocate the dreams and aspirations of women, racial/ethnic minorities, the poor and working class, transgendered and non-gender conforming people, and immigrants. Budding scholars and practitioners will insist on gender and culturally responsive research scholarship that will help them comprehend and combat these political assaults and other social problems.

The book will certainly appeal to researchers interested in qualitative approaches in urban education, gender studies, ethnic studies, anthropology, and research methods courses. In the text, I draw upon critical qualitative inquiry and/or leanings (e.g. personal reflection, auto/ethnography, narrative inquiry, storytelling, poetics, etc.) to engage in meaningful and unapologetic conversations on race, class, gender, sexuality, privilege, and power. I am hesitant to *name* what I am "doing" in this book, but I imagine it as Black feminist/womanist prose and performance. The naming and categorizing that takes place in the social sciences and scientific pursuits has never worked in favor of my people. Thus, I am hesitant to name what I am doing, or what I am at the least attempting to do, in this book, but it is safe to say that most, if not all, of the conversations/performances in the book derive from my experiences as an activist scholar committed to the ideals of critical race (Black/Africana) feminism, intersectionality, and critical qualitative research as inquiry and praxis.

Recently, we are witnessing a growing body of literature on the ways in which culturally and linguistically diverse scholars engage in qualitative inquiry. However, what is absent in qualitative inquiry discussions is a book for "colored girls" from the (neighbor)hood—an academic book situated between Audre Lorde, bell hooks, and Cynthia Dillard. *Black Feminism in Qualitative Inquiry* is written in the aesthetics of Blackness and Black womanhood "speak" that is grounded in a sub/urban experiences. What do I refer to when I write of Blackness and Black woman speak? It means data analysis portrayed as African American English Vernacular or Black English, double-speak, speaking in tongues, Black beauty—styling and profiling, girly pontifications serving up life lessons. Life becomes data; data becomes praxis; praxis becomes awareness; awareness becomes critical consciousness. Word.

Articulated differently, the following informs how I approach life qualitatively:

- **Popular culture**. Engagement with social media, television, movies, magazines, music, etc. shapes my views of the social world. Popular culture inspires but is also an alternative creative form of expression. Today, it is creatively and instantly distributed in sound bites that are easily consumable to everyday people. Research has not been able to be consumed or turned around so easily, especially in ways that are palatable.
- **Rhythm and Blues (R&B)**. Stories in sound that reach that soul, teach about love, and cause one to "jones" informs my understanding of sex, sexuality, sexual identity, romance, disappointments, and ecstasy in intimate and platonic relationships. All this is poetic inspiration.
- **Hip Hop**. As a cultural form of expression and genre of music and a movement, this inspires me to create and perform in rhythms and rhymes. My tastes leans toward urbanism, freshness, colors, beats, uniqueness in expression (I cannot "bite" nobody else's style) while being a part of a whole; defiance, critique, and improvisation. Spoken word and rhyming effects not only what I write but also how I write, navigate, and critique the social world.
- **Humor**. Jokes, sarcasm, or "playing the dozens," "cadding," and "casing" has traditionally been used in the African American tradition and demonstrates wit, critical thinking, and semantic prowess through language games (i.e. double-speak). Humor as affection and linguistic strategy helps to cope emotionally with difficult situations and topics. Undoubtedly, humor is infused throughout my qualitative performances for it is a part of my primary culture and preferred affective and pedagogical maneuvers.

The rawness of my generation's voice is lacking in qualitative research theorizing and texts. Our rawness evolves from: state sanctioned violence and the acknowledgement that we are colonized people on colonized land; the reality of the effects that HIV/AIDS (or the lack of access to affordable healthcare), mass incarceration, and the prison industrial complex has had on our families and community structures; the War on Poverty, the War on Drugs, (re)gentrification, and disinvestment in public education. That rawness born out of a life of consistent contestation is what I am trying to re/present (con)textually in my qualitative pursuits. What Black feminist author Chimamanda Ngozi Adichie has achieved for women in English, I want to achieve for us in qualitative research in the social sciences—that feeling of inscribed freedom.

What does inscribed freedom look like in the data analysis process? Conversations with the ancestors, deliberations with elders, ritual and ceremony, rite of passages, youth-centered pedagogy, and even the rejection of Eurocentric western notions of time and space. We need qualitative research texts that excite hope for the researcher and researched. Fortunately, most university faculty like myself, who teach qualitative research courses, we prefer influential research texts alongside contemporary texts that are representative of diverse cultural experiences and contexts. It is becoming more and more difficult to find well-written qualitative research texts that stretch the imagination beyond the White educated middle-class male experience, or the White middle-class educated White female feminist experience. There is a need more for qualitative projects that *play in the dark*, sort of speak.

I posit that there remains a need for academic texts that center, amplify, and politicize the everyday lived experiences and multiple identities of Black women (and girls) in the U.S. and across the African Diaspora. I believe it is through stories, personal reflections, and a shared consciousness with marginalized communities that researchers who embrace a qualitative tradition are able to appreciate individuals and a group's full humanity. In this moment of Black Lives Matter and Say Her Name, and Afrofeminism futures, I unabashedly redefine myself as the Black girl cultural historian. Most of us in the field of sociology, education, gender studies, cultural and ethnic studies are bombarded with numbers and statistics that serve to (1) sort and categorize human beings, (2) predict human behavior and social phenomena with the intent of making human beings' interactions and relationships more organized, efficient, and, at times, profitable.

Consequently, critical race scholars have extensively discussed the limitations and potential dangers of quantitative research for the oppressed. And, for quite some time there have been consistent conversations amongst qualitative researchers on the possibilities of qualitative methods for attempting to both portray the experiences of marginalized groups and contend with the inherited tensions in researching "the other." I am interested in playing within that (dark) liminal space between the possibilities of and methodological tensions in qualitative inquiry. How do we declare what counts as data? What are the un/disclosed rituals we partake in the interpretation of data? What happens when we analyze the small print, footnotes, and data on the cutting room floor? What might such revived data tell us about the inherent moral and ethical fallacies of the scientific truth across-the-board? How might an Africana (un)conscious *educe* critical qualitative processes and products grounded in struggles for self-determination, agency, resilience, and resistance?

In fact, I believe that all scholarly endeavors, including research and teaching, should be culturally affirming and forthcoming as far as socio-political intent. Accordingly, readers (or the research audience) will undoubtedly be allowed the opportunity to examine my own motives as a researcher, writer, and pedagogue; throughout the text

I share many personal and professional experiences that inform my research questions, modes of analysis, interpretations, and cultural understandings of what even counts as data and knowledge.

In the spirit of a Black/Africana womanist consciousness, I craft stories, personal narrative, and other forms of creative writing to portray Black woman-centered qualitative inquiry as socio-political praxis. It is through a set of lived experiences, research endeavors, and observations of the social world that I have come to (a) make assumptions about the social world, (b) challenge grand narratives, and (c) question taken-for-granted knowledge about the "other." A few questions raised from the reading of the book as a qualitative project are:

1. How might an Africana feminist epistemology and a critical race, gender, and class-consciousness inform qualitative inquiry?
2. How can we represent the "extraordinary" in the mundane, or in the ordinary ponderings of a Black woman's interpretations of her life and that of other women and girls' lives that surround her?
3. Are qualitative researchers prepared to grapple with a Black woman scholar's admittance that researching the other is bordering on voyeurism, exploitation, and grounded in forms of (race, class, age, and language) privilege? Or, do only certain scholars (i.e. the White, educated, English-speaking elite) get to participate in qualitative conversations about validity and legitimation?
4. Lastly, how do we write up women of African ancestry's herstories, intimate and formal relationships, labor, leisure activities, traditions, habits of mind, ideologies, desires, and disappointments in ways that our experiences are connected to other human experiences and political proclivities across cultural and geographic contexts?

FIELDNOTE 1

A MOSAIC OF BLACK FEMINISM

The fact that racial politics and indeed racism are pervasive factors in our lives did not allow us, and still does not allow most Black women, to look more deeply into our own experiences, and from that sharing and growing consciousness, to build a politics that will change our lives and inevitably end our oppression. Our development must also be tied to the contemporary economic and political position of Black people ... Although our economic position is still at the very bottom of the American capitalistic economy, a handful of us have been able to gain certain tools as a result of tokenism in education and employment which potentially enables us to more effectively fight our oppression.

~*The Combahee River Collective, 1977*

My grandmother was a pretty sophisticated woman. She was born in Mississippi, but she spoke and walked like she was the Queen of England. For years, I would get frustrated with her, because when someone of importance called—no doubt, a White person—she would change her speech to sound like she was from Europe somewhere. I don't simply mean she sounded "White," I mean she actually spoke in a different tone of voice. She presented like an actress!

In Chicago, she dressed in fine clothes, fancy wigs, and beautiful jewelry. She would hold and smoke her cigarette like a lady, and blow smoke to the side or up in the air like a lady. Grandma carried a gun in her purse and slept with one in her bedside drawer. Hell, grandma even liked going to the "lounge" or what we call nightclubs today.

But at church, which we didn't go to very often, grandma would open the hymn book and hum off tune. It would piss me off to high heaven! Grandma was perfect at everything, but she could not keep up with the hymns. All the children noticed it, and we would giggle about it or laugh about it when she was out of earshot.

Then, one day, actually her birthday, she asked me to read a birthday card out loud for her. Being the daughter that I was, I said aloud, "Why can't you read it yourself?" My grandmother simply giggled. There was something about the expression on grandma's face, the backdrop of the giggle, that made her seem more weak than strong in that moment (it would be the first of two times in my life that I witnessed a sign of weakness on her face; the second would be me soaping her back in a warm bath as she wept, weakened by radiation for lung cancer).

On grandma's birthday, the answer to my accidental observation of grandma's facial expression came later on during the car ride home from grandma's house; my aunt said to me matter factly, "You know your grandma can't read!"

No, I did not know. I should have been ashamed in that moment, but I was not. I was actually proud. How in the world did my grandmother, on the south side of Chicago, raise six kids, own her own home as a single parent, and be a community organizer and a nurse? Yes, my grandmother was a nurse!

I later learned that my grandmother, after leaving the South and having to survive on her own, typed up a fake nursing diploma. So, yes, I was proud that my grand-mother defied the odds and tricked the system—patriarchy, White supremacy, and the intelligentsia—she did what she had to do to survive. Once I learned of her secret, which was around the age of 12, I not only admired her strength and cle-verness, I revered it. Grandma's strength, beauty, grace, and intelligence is what I aspire to be. She's my spirit guide, because she used what she already embodied and what she did know to CREATE.

Revelation: Grandma's gun and "fanciness" were basically her *tools* for navigating across different cultural communities.

In this book, I use the term Black feminism to describe a long tradition of Black women's intellectual labor and community endeavors in the U.S. and across the African Diaspora. Although most scholars interested in Black women's approaches to qualitative inquiry are able to define Black feminism and locate it within a larger intellectual tradition within the social science and critical theory, we do not always agree that it is appropriate or accurate to lump the body of Black women's political struggles inside and outside the academy as "Black feminism," or, for that matter, for Black women who participate in gender-centered scholarly pursuits or community engagement, to be identified as a "feminist" or as a "Black feminist."

At this moment in history, we are witnessing first hand a resurgence of Black women, youth, and other subjugated groups boldly and actively resisting mainstream institutions' discourse, language, and concepts associated with the oppressor class. Black women like myself who are born within or enculturated into an African-centered community, or young women educated on an African consciousness, are taught to conscientiously question, resist, and reject ideologies and taken-for-granted assumptions handed down by White scholars or those trained in Eurocentric paradigms. Feminism as a term and as an ideology is no exception. Feminism is a range of political ideologies, social and political move-ments that call for political, economic, and social equity between the sexes.

More than 20 years after being introduced to the term and ideas of (White liberal) feminism as an undergraduate student, I persistently ask: What is feminism and what does it mean for Black women and girls? Who is a feminist and how will the label "feminist" validate or invalidate my own credibility as a Black woman scholar and community activist? And, what do Black women compromise when we align with feminism, especially since it is viewed as a theoretical and political agenda *belonging to* liberal White women? Even more, is *Black* simply being added to the term feminism to make (White women's) feminism more palatable to non-White women, or are Black scholars simply adding *Black* to feminism to represent the addition of race politics to gender politics? As an institutionalized (and commodified) concept, Black feminism as intellectual thought is certainly familiar, but certainly is contested as a discourse. Language is power and the power to name is just as powerful!

Intellectual migrations

Therefore, to critical scholars, especially those engaged in decolonial thinking and who critique the social world from an Afrocentric episteme like myself, Black feminism at first glance appears to be like the "lions dancing with the hunters." However, as long as we choose to play within the confines of Western institutions and with an adopted language (i.e. academic English), Black women will always compromise, negotiate, and balance the needs of institutions and our struggles for social, economic, political, and education liberation. Participation in the politics of language does not give way to concession. For instance, in the U.S., those of African ancestry have historically struggled with naming ourselves as a cultural and political group. A few cultural/political names that have emerged over the last century or so: Colored, Negro, African American, African, Black, Black American, and African in America.

Some of these names have been forced upon us while others have been adopted or adapted. I contend here that (1) the English language is limited and unimaginative, and (2) as Black/African we name ourselves within a larger socio-political context. This is understood when naming ourselves as an ethnic and cultural group situated within a particular geopolitical context(s). Therefore, we need to be careful of coloring Black women's ponderings of "our naming" as frivolous or moreover as a thoughtless concession to White women's (epistemic) domination.

I am Black and African, and my mother bestowed upon me my Earth name, Venus. Beyond given familial names, cultural/ethnic/political identities are too naturally fluid. For example, while serving in South Africa, I was often described, when introduced or in conversation, as *American* or *an American Black*. I was shaken to the core when my American identity was forefronted in South Africa by other Africans, because I rarely considered myself as American. In contrast to the South African context, in the U.S., I was always *Black or African American*. Never was I told that I was American first and then Black or African. This naming did not fit my constitution.

As another example, once a dear friend and adopted family member in her native tongue described me to an elder, who did not speak English and with little contact with city life, as *half-caste*. In other words, in their minds, I was not authentically or wholly "African"! Nonetheless, I explained to my peer, who was also my adopted sister, that culturally and politically I align with the continent and people of Africa, and that spiritually I am situated (read: axiologically speaking) and "called" (read: ontologically speaking) back to my ancestral land. Intellectually speaking, my worldview migrates back and forth, in between, and across continents, histories, and diverse religious and spiritual traditions, and political orientations.

As a matter of fact, Western science would never accept an African womanist worldview where the "subject" herself claims to transcend time and place, or a worldview where the notion of time and place are themselves scientific constructions open to critique, questioning, and manipulation. In South Africa, Ghana, North America, and across the African Diaspora, we all are (re)learning to name ourselves for ourselves. As hinted at above, the naming of ourselves is inevitably hindered by language, discursive boundaries and power, and geopolitical context. Yet, our naming does not negate our endeavors to analytically frame our social, political, economic, cultural, and philosophical contestations.

Black feminism is not my naming, but mostly my "framing" of my racial *and* sexual politics. As an example of *framing* vs. *naming*, my aunt, sister, and I have the same picture of my maternal grandmother hanging or sitting on shelves in each of our homes. And although we all have the same picture of my grandmother, adorned in a blue outfit with decorative pearl earrings and a matching necklace, the picture is of a different size (e.g. 8 x 5 or 10 x 12) and we all have different frames that accentuate and forefront her image. The different frames do not distort our memories of her nor distort the constitution of the picture. This is how I, in fact, view Black feminism and other similarly situated theoretical frameworks like African feminism, African womanism, Pan African womanism, and womanism. Depending on our location in the world and particular body of politics, Black women scholars borrow different language(s) and/or "frames" to accentuate and forefront our memories and lived realities based on personal tastes, aesthetics, and convenience.

For me, I support the ideals of Black feminism while also, awkwardly at times, rejecting being labeled as a Black feminist. Although I do align with anti-racism and gender equity, and fervently engage in resistance efforts against White supremacy patriarchy capitalism imperialism, which is consistent with Black feminism as theory and praxis, Black feminism as institutionalized knowledge (and now a part of popular discourse) has been commodified and co-opted to a point that it might be too "centered" for my tastes. Meaning, I am reluctant to identify with any given identity that has become so accepted by the status quo that it no longer poses a real or perceived threat to dominant discourse, hegemonic structures, or social groups aligned with authoritarianism.

On the other hand, reluctance to name aside, centering Black feminism in this conversation about qualitative inquiry allow us a shared starting point, which centers Black women's epistemology, approaches to analysis, analyzing, critique, and interpretations of the social world. Accepting the limitation of an institutionalized Black feminism while also imagining its futures, I present Black feminism as a mosaic. Black women across the diaspora have shared the unique history of surviving and struggling against White supremacy, economic oppression and domination, and gender oppression. How do we reflect upon these shared histories to carve out theoretical and methodological spaces of our own? Black women interested in the lives of Black women, have much, herstorical, theoretical, and practical knowledge to contribute to contemporary qualitative inquiry and discourse.

Many of us were introduced to the idea of "scientific research" by White men, and later the concept of qualitative research by White women, while reading assigned texts of White researchers' interpretations of the social world and experiences. Consequently, our understanding of qualitative inquiry begins and too often ends from a White-centric lens. It is imperative that those committed to social and racial justice paradigms give attention to how non-White women make sense of contemporary and historical patterns. Moreover, it is equally important for us to consider the ways in which Black women seek to question, understand, and challenge, via the formal inquiry process, contemporary social injustice, like the imposition of deficit-thinking, white supremacy, and racialized gender bias in society as well as the research process itself.

In the past, qualitative research has been metaphorically described as a bricolage, a montage, quilt-making, and musical improvisation. In this fieldnote, I would like to describe Black feminism, and specifically its possibilities to qualitative research, as a mosaic. Mosaic as an artform is the process of creating images with an assortment of small pieces of colored glass, stone, or other objects put together to create a pattern or picture. In most instances, the mosaic has cultural and spiritual significance. Black feminist scholars bring a wealth of knowledge, skills, talents, and experiences into the research process. These bits of experiences mold together to construct our multiple identities. And, from these multiple identities, yields a creative, distinctly mosaic worldview.

Using the metaphor of a mosaic, a piece of artwork composed of a combination of diverse elements, patterns, and forms, I propose a gender- and race-based approach to qualitative inquiry and analysis, alongside an inevitable critique of capitalism and economic exploitation. Black women scholars have a long tradition of facilitating knowledge of the connection between culture and theory formation. Throughout the text, I put forth the stance that due to continually navigating the contours of racism, classism, and sexism by virtue of existing in the confines of the matrix of White domination, women of African ancestry offer unique perspectives on the ways in which inequality persists within and across cultural contexts and institutions.

In the following discussion, the tenets and methodology of Black feminism/ womanism are explained in relation to qualitative research methods and analysis. Also discussed is the usefulness of Black feminism to expose and trouble marginalization and exclusionary practices in qualitative inquiry. It is argued that a researcher's embracement of a Black feminist consciousness shapes: (1) musings about knowledge and knowing, (2) how one interacts with participants throughout the research process, (3) one's understanding of the context where the study takes place, (4) the body of literature reviewed, and (5) interpretation and analysis of data.

Although more recently there has been an increase in research conducted with or about women and girls of African descent, this body of research still receives less attention in qualitative research textbooks, in particular when looking at how research is applicable to current social, health, and economic challenges like food insecurity, state sanctioned violence, school inequality, obesity and cancer, childhood trauma, homophobia, etc. Black women's worldview is shaped by our everyday joys and struggles as well as our quests to solve our own community's problems and pushback against societal barriers.

To echo Ladson-Billings (2000):

> The process of developing a worldview that differs from the dominant worldview requires active intellectual work on the part of the knower, because schools, society, and the structure and production of knowledge are designed to create individuals who internalize the dominant worldview and knowledge production and acquisition process.
>
> (p. 258)

The mosaic of Black feminism brings forth an aesthetically distinct alternative to widely accepted notions of how knowledge production and acquisition should transpire in qualitative inquiry and analysis.

Multiple consciousness

Black feminism or womanism (a term coined by Alice Walker in 1983 to address the concerns of Black women about the history of racism in the feminist movement) was born out of Black women's experiences and struggles against slavery, U.S. apartheid, and their on-going political involvement in Black and women's liberation movements. As I have articulated elsewhere (Evans-Winters, 2017; Evans-Winters & Love, 2015), in the post-civil rights era, for many, a Black feminist consciousness is developed from (1) hearing family members shared stories of struggles and triumphs against racial oppression, (2) participation in one's own first-hand experiences and continued struggle to spiritually and physically survive de facto segregated spaces, (3) experiences with hyper-surveillance in urban schools and neighborhoods (e.g. racial profiling, metal detectors in schools, drug testing of students, etc.), (4) witnessing symbolic lynchings (e.g. the first Black man president being depicted as a terrorist and monkey, countless Black young men and women killed and their murders being circulated on public television and social media while their murderers are acquitted), (5) militarized public schools (e.g. zero tolerance policies and armed policies officers on school sites), and (6) being allowed in White spaces for the sole intent of "speaking for the race" at a time when affirmative action initiatives are being rolled back in education and employment, leaving many Black women lonely, vulnerable, and absent of community.

Black feminist thought is a reflection of multiple theoretical traditions, including African-centered thought, feminist theory, Marxism, sociology of knowledge, critical social theory, and postmodern theory. Furthermore, Black feminist thought crosses the disciplines of cultural studies, literary studies, education, sociology, economics, political science, history, anthropology, African and African American studies, gender studies, legal studies and law, social work, media studies and the arts (e.g. dance, theater, singing, etc.). Black feminism as it is known today is "a continuation of intellectual and activist traditions" (Guy-Sheftall, 1995, p. 1), as well as African and African American values, beliefs, and traditions. Black feminist scholar Guy-Sheftall (1995) points out that Black feminism is not a monolithic static ideology; however, there are consistent axioms consistent throughout Black feminist thought, including the belief that:

- Black women experience a special kind of oppression, due to their racial and gender identity, and access to limited resources in a racist, sexist, classist society. Guy-Sheftall (1995) refers to the interlocking systems of race, class, and gender oppression that Black women confront as a triple jeopardy.
- The political, social, and intellectual needs of Black women characteristically differ from that of Black men and White women; therefore, strategies of resistance must also differ. Black women must fight for racial and gender synchronously, because of this verity they cannot afford to privilege one group's struggle over the other, for Black liberation will not eradicate patriarchy and the elimination of gender domination will not ineluctably eradicate White supremacy.
- Black women's commitment to challenging racism and sexism is rooted in their lived experience as Black and woman.

Black feminism as theory and praxis is propitious to qualitative researchers. Black feminism is a critical social theory born out of the lived experiences and struggles of Black women living at the intersections of race, class, and gender oppression. Indubitably, Black feminism as a tradition of Black women's intellectual thought is devalued and marginalized in qualitative methods courses and textbooks. Conversely, White men scholars are apotheosized as founders of qualitative inquiry in general, and White women as "doers" of feminist qualitative research.

Oversight of Black women's contributions to qualitative research can be attributed to scholars not knowing or willing to acknowledge Black people as scientists and theorists, lack of awareness of Black women as producers of knowledge, and a tradition of racial and gender exclusion in the academy. Regrettably, both of the aforementioned reasons can lead historians and scholars of qualitative research to overlook or downplay Black women's role in the evolution of qualitative inquiry and discourse.

Black women's cemented status at the bottom of the social hierarchy enkindles a unique vantage point for the critique, analysis, and interpretation of sexist gender socialization and racial oppression. Our approach to qualitative data analysis is no ordinary magic; it's grounded in ancestral knowledge, history, art, and formal education. Black feminist theorist bell hooks (2000), in *Feminist Theory: From Margin to Center*, "There is much evidence substantiating the reality that race and class identity creates differences in quality of life, social status, and lifestyle that take precedence over the common experience women share – differences that are rarely transcended" (p. 4). Black women as researchers, and the researched, bring our lived realities into the research process. The charge of the qualitative researcher, then, is to add to the body of evidence that already exists about different groups of women and the genders; to descriptively capture and illustrate the nuanced differences between groups of women's social and material conditions; and, to bring forth alternative analyses for referencing gender and racial oppression. Inevitably, Black feminist thought transforms the purpose and discourse of qualitative inquiry.

Crafting race, class, and gender into qualitative inquiry

Black feminism is a theoretical, methodological, and political discourse steeped in a tradition that centers the voices of Black women's socio-political struggles in a White supremacist capitalist patriarchal imperialist society that privileges Whiteness, maleness, and wealth. Black feminism has an unabating concern for addressing the needs of non-White women and the poor. As a critical theory, Black feminism yields a theoretical frame for understanding how racism, sexism, ableism, adultism, xenophobia, homophobia, and classism intersect to constrain women's bodies and psyches.

Moreover, Black feminism as a standpoint theory, also offers original suppositions into how Black women are able to confront the social world order, while being simultaneously vulnerable and resilient in the face of systematic inequality, including marginalization in the academy. Black feminist anthropologist Leith Mullings (1997) writes in the book, *On our own terms: Race, class, and gender in the lives of African American women,* in our quest to set the record straight, "To only focus on the strengths, accomplishments, and victories does not give sufficient attention to the system of domination. Yet to emphasize too heavily the structure of oppression underplays the creative energy of a people" (p. xii). In our knowledge pursuits to set the record straight, symmetry is in our tellings of oppression and resistance is fundamental. Black feminism reminds researchers that Black women have the right to assert our rights and to demand rights. This reminder repurposes qualitative inquiry and informs data analysis.

Hence, Mullings' (1997) assertion above reminds those of us committed to writing women's lives to conscientiously interweave into our observations, interpretations, and theoretical ponderings stories of individual and collective agency, resilience, resistance, and celebrations. Such an interweaving creates a mosaicism of possibility, which can serve as a theoretical and heuristic guide for researchers interested in racial justice, gender equity, human rights, and social harmony. Methodologically, Black feminism offers researchers, especially women of color, a culturally congruent and politically legitimate lens and set of methods for analyzing Black girls and women's, indigenous women, poor women, and other colonized people's cultures and histories. Articles, autobiographies, sounds, comedies, fictions, narratives, and tales are all open for analysis through a Black feminist lens. All together these tellings are our mosaic and are tangible representations of our epistemological assumptions and orientations.

Politically, Black feminism is an intentional political disruption to conventional (Eurocentric, Western) academic descant and colonial teachings propagated as "science." Accordingly, a major modus operandi of Black feminism is the intellectual practice of claiming the margins.

When in the 1970s and 1980s Black women and other similarly situated groups broke long-standing silences about their oppression, they spoke from the margins of power. Moreover, by claiming historically marginalized experiences, they effectively challenged false universal knowledge that historically defended hierarchical power relations. Marginality operated as an important site of resistance for decentering unjust power relations.

(Collins, 2000, pp. 43–44)

Black feminist researchers center Black women's experiential knowledge, thus, concomitantly disrupt universal truths. Collins' coinage of oppositional knowledge describes Black women's scholarly commitment to (re)claiming and (re)defining our "place" in society and academia. In African-centered women's use of qualitative research, we strive to shift conversations on the lives of Black women away from mere conversations on victimization and powerlessness to piecing together the representations of our lives as a mosaic of intellectual creativity and a praxis of resistance.

Black feminism in qualitative inquiry offers the opportunity to expose and challenge the complex relationship between science and domination; Black women's history of subjectification and objectification; metanarratives; and everyday folklore and myths (Payne, 1984) produced and proliferated by dominant institutions in reproducing social inequality. Black feminist thought in qualitative analysis: (1) proffers a social critique of traditional research paradigms and tralatitious interpretations of social relationships; (2) fosters dialogue for understanding unmitigated power and privilege; and (3) strategically agitates the status quo. Once again, on a note on the significance of Black feminist anthropology, Mullings (1997) emphasizes that "Science, including social science, is practiced in the context of society; it is influenced by the power relationships of a given society, and knowledge (or what passes for knowledge) may be used as an instrument for subjugation or liberation," (p. 77). Black feminism magnifies both the intricacies and complexities of power relationships—this magnification is our mosaic—which we use in pursuits of scientific knowledge for liberation.

Today, there are a numerous topics that may be of interest to qualitative researchers that adopt a Black feminist stance, such as Black girls' experiences in their families, communities, and schools; Black women's resistance efforts in the movement for Black lives (i.e. Black Lives Matter); the experiences of Black women educators as school teachers and administrators; street harassment and rape culture; Black women's experiences in higher education; teacher educators' experience with teaching race/racism; girls' educational and social development across the African diaspora; Black parental engagement in and perceptions of schools and schooling; Black female pre-Kindergarten-12 administrators; community activism for educational reform; gender and the school to prison pipeline, Black women's preparation for the post-industrial marketplace; Black women's experiences in STEM education and careers; Black women's work and participation in alternative learning communities; literacy programs and gender and culturally relevant curriculum and pedagogy, Black girls' peer relationships; representations of Black girls and women in popular culture; Black women's art as activism and pedagogy; gender and educational law, theology and educational theory; the education of Black women athletes; gender and race socialization in schools. What is the role of qualitative researchers in bringing attention to inequality, mitigating epistemic apartheid, decolonizing knowledge or interrupting Eurocentric Western profligacy? In *Black Feminism in Qualitative Inquiry*, we (the collective "I") approach the complexity of life at the margins and in the intersections.

A mosaic of Black feminist thought

> A lot of us do not understand what it really would take to make our work available to the next generation—not only for those who follow us to read about what we believed and valued and tried to do with our living, but also to receive our stories as models and the base from which our children may move in the world they struggle to shape. The idea that the world you live in is one you should work to shape moves across time only if it is a part of the cultural environment you create and put in motion. (Reagon, 1993, p. 207)

The above-mentioned civil rights activist and historian, Bernice Johnson Reagon, calls for intentional attention to document and disseminate the cultural histories and perceptions of Black women getting the story right for the next generation of scholars, practitioners, students, and policymakers. A new generation of qualitative researchers are bestowed the privilege of reconstructing others' perceptions of Black people, women, and people living in poverty. Black feminism in qualitative inquiry provides a mosaic for synchronously reconstructing and co-constructing the values, ethos, and worldviews that have helped to sustain our cultural knowledge, rituals, and traditions. Unlike many of our researching counterparts, we do not have the privilege or luxury of writing and researching for the sake of pleasure or monetary rewards. Citizens and other members of our kinship communities are being shot down in the street by state actors and White vigilantes, Black young women and other women of color are being incarcerated at historic rates, and too many children are pushed out of the school house to the jail house. Next, I demonstrate how Black women construct a mosaic of knowledge to combat urgent dehumanizing social ills.

Reflections and oppositional knowledge construction

Black women's (as the researcher and researched) experiences are at the center of analysis in the qualitative research process informed by Black feminist thought. The Black feminist qualitative researcher begins with reflections on her own lived experiences and brings those insights into the research process. She does not claim to be an expert on a particular research topic or subject; however, she does view her observations of the social world just as significant to the research process as that of other researchers and other participants in the research process. Black feminist qualitative research challenges the perception that research is or needs to be conclusively objective and alternatively presupposes that all scientific claims are subjective.

Black feminism's qualitative pursuits must be in direct opposition to Eurocentric Western, male-centered hegemonic knowledge claims and practices. Historically, Black women have served as objects of so-called science and as scientific commentary; therefore, Black women know unequivocally that science is not always objective in its purposes or consequences. Evidence of science as a technology of the state and tool of White supremacy includes a U.S. government led and privately funded the eugenics movement, medical experimentation and sterilization of Black young women and other women of color (Roberts, 1997), and the 1965 Moynihan report that colored the Black family and mother as sloven and negligent. From a critical Black woman's stance, eugenics ideology lives in the popular imagination and it is the undercurrent of much of scientific thought.

In agreement with Angrosino and Mays de Perez (2000):

> Whatever else may be said about the postmodern turn in contemporary studies of society and culture, its critique of assumptions about the objectivity of science and its presumed authoritative voice has raised issues that all qualitative researchers need to address. Earlier criticism might have been directed at particular researchers, with the question being whether they had lived up to the expected standards of objective scholarship. In the postmodern milieu, by contrast, the criticism is directed at the standards themselves. In effect, it is now possible to question whether observational objectivity is either desirable or feasible as a goal. (p. 109)

A questioning of the objectivity of science and the purpose of science coincides with critical qualitative research paradigms. However, we are skeptical of postmodern turns that proclaim that research is *nothing but everything*! It is only everything when their voice is centered or their modality of inquiry is applauded. The inclination that research and writing is only meaningful in and of itself is derived from a place of privilege; the researcher/researchered and her audience must breathe life into the study of society and culture to bring forth its meaningfulness (as possibility and action) to the dispossessed.

Black women and other indigenous scholars have long questioned the objectivity of science, scientists' political and individual motives, and the utility of the scientific process itself. Furthermore, Black feminists have always proclaimed, for personal and political reasons, that objectivity in the critique of society is neither desirable nor feasible in ongoing efforts to employ systematic investigation methods in combating White supremacy and male domination. Black feminism maintains that qualitative inquiry with culturally and linguistically diverse individuals and communities at the center of analysis is axiomatically political and subjective with the intent of promoting social change, self-knowledge and empowerment, and community uplift.

Dialogical voice(s) as discursive activism

Sojourner Truth and Maria Stewart are two public pioneers who brought the concernments of Black women's expressiveness to the forefront of race and gender liberation discussions (hooks, 2000; Giddings, 2014; Davis, 2011). In the pursuit of self-determination, Black women have relied on creative and alternative ways of constructing and legitimating knowledge claims that serve to portray our shared socio-political cultural experiences. The embracement of a dialogical voice in the conception and pursuance of knowledge is a result of Black women's participation in communal and civic spaces (Collins, 1998) like religious institutions, fraternal organizations, and political groups (Davis, 1993). These organizations tend to be more democratic in nature and organization.

Therefore, it is commonplace for many who take on a Black feminist standpoint to use personal narratives, to share personal conversations, or symbols and metaphors as a way to convey information or to question the validity of knowledge claims (Dillard, 2000). To this point, Carol Lee (2005, p. 83) content that people in the African Diaspora,

> have a highly embedded appreciation of language play, a love of playing with language as an aesthetic end in itself, as opposed to a strict utilitarian tool of communication. Use of rhythm, alliteration, metaphor, irony, and satire are routine in the language practices of this speech community.

This assertion is noteworthy because in the text *Black Education: A Transformative Research and Action Agenda for the New Century*, King (2005) lays out a progressive agenda for the improvement of Black education. Progressive in the sense that research is reflective of the languages, histories, cultures, spirituality, and experiences of the African Diaspora; and transformative research is action-oriented (or outcome-based). The outcome(s) can be a *witnessed* change in attitude (e.g. becoming aware that Black girls are punished in schools at higher rates than their White male and female counterparts), behavior (e.g. reducing the number of Black girls receiving out-of-school suspensions), or policy (e.g. removing police officers from school buildings). A progressive research agenda in Black feminist qualitative inquiry is a "witnessing." In the analysis process, in the call and response tradition, we are metaphorically asking, "Can I get a witness?"

Therefore, it is significant to note that language and literacy is a worthwhile topic of discussion in qualitative inquiry and social activism. Speech in the African and African American tradition, in written or oral form, is regarded as a creative and divine act. Speech, which does include the skill of listening, is used to pass down tradition and preserve the culture (Carruthers, 1999). Once more, speech is not to be taken lightly or as apolitical.

For this reason, in the African/American intellectual tradition, a dialogical voice (the act of listening, writing, and conversing in one's cultural point of reference) is preferred in Black feminist methodology as opposed to the use of insipid scientific language. Scientific jargon can be exclusionary, while privileging formally educated, middle-class, and Eurocentric styles and patterns of speech. Similarly, narration in the form of storytelling, metaphors, and analogies is more relational in nature; thus, inherently dialogical. There is an attempt at mutuality in questioning, observing, theorizing, and contemplating one's interactions with the social world.

Stated differently, "The narrative approach entails a distinct type of research, but over and above that it comprises a clear vision of the social world and the way we think, feel and conduct ourselves in it" (Spector-Mersel, 2010, p. 209). The narrative approach is not simply a qualitative research technique but a research strategy. Accordingly, narrative voice undergirded with Black women's sensibilities and ontoepistemologies (i.e. oral history, storytelling, biography, etc.) sets out to paint a picture of Black women's perceptions of the social world order and how they might choose to respond to such (dis)order. Black women's narrative traditions become narrative literacies in critical Black feminist qualitative analysis. Black women's narrative literacies are important humanizing projects in contemporary contexts that attempt to dehumanize, oppress, suppress, and annihilate Black bodies.

Accordingly, one objective of dialogical approaches in Black feminist inquiry is to arrive at democratic shared understandings of a social problem, with the conclusive objective of collectively imagining how to solve identified social problems or scourged social structures. Another objective of the use of narratives in Black feminist writing is to provide counterstories to racist and patriarchal portrayals of indigenous women and people, especially those stories that have been detrimental to Black women. With the recent rise in popularity and embracement of critical race theory and critical race feminism, there is also more awareness of the utility of counter-narratives in countering racial and gender oppression in law (see Wing, 1997, for an overview of critical race feminism in the legal field) and in educational research (Ladson-Billings & Tate, 1995; Evans-Winters & Esposito, 2010; Taylor, Gillborn, & Ladson-Billings, 2009; Lynn & Dixson, 2013).

Lastly, a narrative voice allows for the acceptance of emotion in knowledge acquisition and counterclaims. An ethics of care and empathy are important in qualitative inquiry and in the assessment of the validity of an exposition. The dichotomy between rationality and emotionality is obscured in Black feminist inquiry and data analysis. If the messenger is absent of emotion or fails to capture and keep the attention of the receiver of the message, the message itself might be lost or the messenger may be dismissed as less than credible. Scholars who embrace the tenets of Black feminism have also embraced this intellectual challenge of keeping a strong presence of emotional investment visible.

Of course, issues of credibility and legitimacy are ongoing points of contention in qualitative research. Black feminist methodological approaches emerge at the liminal of interminable paradigmatic wars in academia. The crisis of legitimacy (Denzin & Lincoln, 2000) in qualitative educational research is between foundationalism, positivism and postpositivism, postfoundationalism, critical theory, postmodernism, and postructuralism. Black feminist truth claims are deemed to be credible within our communities, and our "truths" must be validated from within, with less concern for how outsiders legitimate (or receive and perceive) our assertions. Black women's lived experiences, and reflections of these socially constructed experiences, are legitimate subjects of research and analysis.

My litmus test? Would my grandmother view this research as worthwhile? Can my godmother understand what it is I am arguing and believe the argument is worth sharing? Can my sister hear my voice when she reads my stories, narratives, and musings, or would she proclaim that I am full of it and I have taken on someone's else's voice and words? Finally, could my daughter be able to explain my observations and interpretations and recommendations to a policymaker? In other words, these decolonizing liberatory projects start at home with Black women's knowledges, imaginations, and performances of inquiry and analyses.

(Con)textual multiplicity

Black feminism is with concerned critical methodologies that are accessible and palatable to diverse audiences, with a special objective of including women, men, and youth in the struggle against White supremacy and male domination while grappling with epistemic apartheid (Rabaka, 2010). "If feminist writing and scholars aim to promote and advance feminist movement, then matters of style must be considered in conjunction with political intent. There will be no feminist movement as long as feminist ideas are understood only by an educated few," states bell hooks (2000, p. 113). One of the most effective means for conveying a feminist agenda to both those a part of and outside of formal educational institutions, as well as those turned off from various feminist theories, is by integrating non-traditional texts or a multiplicity of texts into scientifically informed writings.

I posit here that data analysis engages a multiplicity of texts in Black feminist qualitative inquiry. These *texts* become the makeup of our mosaic. Certainly, the idea of what is considered text is itself scrutinized. In the analysis of *texts*, in Black feminist qualitative inquiry, we might ponder: How does a piece of literary work (e.g. novels, poetry, oral histories, biographies, biblical verse, etc.) or cultural artifact like a photograph make a meaningful contribution to interpretations of Black women's existence? How can film and other media images counter commonly held stereotypes and racial tropes? How do musical lyrics proliferate misogyny and sexism, or poor relationships between Black women and men?

Historically, for instance, how has hip hop culture brought women's voices, power, self-determination into conversations about sexual agency, gender performances, and Black women's aesthetics? How can popular media, including social media, be used as a vehicle for educating the masses on interlocking systems of oppression and to mobilize the public? What role has the White corporate media elite played in recycling and propagandizing the superiority and inferiority of different groups in society? Because mainstream knowledge has traditionally excluded Black women from participation in knowledge production, or constructed narrow images of women and non-Whites, often for Black and women scholars it is essential to turn outside of institutionalized knowledge and pivot toward alternative texts (i.e. data sources) for the examination of social phenomenon, relationships, and cultural contexts.

Again, simply because something or someone has not been legitimized by academe does not mean that person, idea, or place is not worthwhile to involve in knowledge (re) construction. For instance, even the human body can serve as text. Collins (2004), for example, in *Black Sexual Politics: African Americans, Gender and the New Racism*, provides a historical overview of White Europeans' objectification of the Black woman's body, especially the rear end, for scientific exploitation and commodification. In the analysis process, Collins connected historical patterns of conquest and control to present-day media images and the exploitation of Black women's body parts to illustrate how sound bites can distort images of Black women for others' consumption and material gains.

Like Collins' analysis demonstrates above, in the mosaic of Black feminist qualitative inquiry performances, everyday taken-for-granted images, symbols, artifacts, gestures, and languages serve as reflections of human behavior and relationships; thus, all of the aforementioned plus many more cultural practices can inform social scientists about social and cultural conditions. Existing at the intersections of race, class, and gender, Black women bring multiple perspectives to the research process; therefore, Black women's objects of analysis, tools of analysis, and approaches to analysis will also be multifarious. Our objects/tools/approaches to analysis centers politics of Black consciousness and Black liberation.

For example, visual art, fiction, drama, poetry, music, and storytelling are creative and culturally congruent with Black women's ways of *sharing* experience and conveying messages. Ntozake Shange, Alice Walker, and Toni Morrison; Nina Simone, Lauryn Hill, and Beyoncé, Gwendolyn Brooks and Zora Neal Hurston are just a few Black women artists whom have presented in alternative textual forms the daily struggles Black women endure from conjointly race-based and gendered perspectives. With critical Black feminism, qualitative researchers have the opportunity to politically collaborate and disseminate our observations and interpretations with more culturally and linguistically diverse audiences. From a critical standpoint, I believe that it is an opportune time for qualitative researchers to use ideas and knowledge acquired from our interpretations of the social world and lived realities to mobilize the masses against hegemony and despotism inside and outside of academia.

Theory and praxis

Admittedly, a White woman told me what *feminism is*, but it was my grandmother who showed me how *Black feminists live*. My grandmother planted the soil of pro-woman/ pro-Black/pro-Black Woman long before I entered a higher education classroom; however, a White woman in a lecture hall in undergraduate school planted the seed of women's liberation. And, even before that undergraduate lecture hall, it was a White woman teacher who suggested that I read the autobiography of Nelson Mandela. Ironically, it was my grandmother's strength and tenacity embedded in my very constitution that made me return to that same teacher and make the requests to read the biography of Winnie Mandela. I wanted to know Winnie Mandela's life as Black African woman revolutionary. How did a Black woman learn to *organize* and *fight* against apartheid? I needed to know these revolutionaries' methodologies of resistance!

The above reflection unmasks the evolution of my own theoretical sensibilities and my deep-seated devotedness to putting ideas into action. A concern for ideas and action is not uncommon for those with Black feminist leanings. Furthermore, as hooks (2000, p. 115) reminds us warrior spirits,

> By dismissing theory and privileging organization work, some women of color are able to see themselves as more politically engaged where it really counts. Yet by buying into this dichotomy between theory and practice, we place ourselves always on the side of the experiential, and in so doing support the notion (too often fostered by white women) that their role is to do the "brain" work, developing ideas, theories, etc., while our role is to do either the dirty work or to contribute the experience to validate and document their analysis.

For Black women and other women of color researchers, it is important to weave together theory and organizational work without privileging one form of labor over another. Better yet, from a qualitative research perspective, our very existence becomes are our sites of observation and analysis—we want to play in between the lines of the experiential and theorized. Then, in community with other women and people of color we have a responsibility to ensure that theory moves beyond the confines of the White (ivory) tower and facilitates change at the personal and/ or micro-, meso-, and macro-levels. Of course, it is important for critical qualitative researchers to engage theory; however, it is just as important for us to explore the ways in which our theoretical pronouncements might be used to resist all forms of oppression and to foster equanimity of the genders and sexes, racial justice, and human rights. Moreover, Black women and other non-White women must recognize that they have the knowledge-base, skill-set, and cultural intuition—and I would add, ancestral wisdom—to "do theory."

Another important theme consistent with Black feminism as praxis is Black women's historical legacy of connecting social reform to consciousness-raising via education with Black students in formal and informal settings. Consciousness-raising takes place in different settings, such as classrooms, prisons, community centers, churches and mosques, theaters, etc. More recently, social media is playing a greater role in both knowledge production and knowledge consumption of Black women's intellectual projects, for instance. All of these alternative spaces potentially become conduits for the Black feminist qualitative researcher's observations, documentations, analysis, and performances.

A framing of the pieces

If "analyzing and creating imaginative responses to injustice characterizes the core of Black feminist thought" (Collins, 2000, p. 12), then the mosaicism of how Black feminist qualitative researchers analyze "data," and decide what counts as data; and how we creatively give testimony to our own multiple realities and others' lived experiences can characterize the future of Black feminist qualitative inquiry.

Conversely, how Black feminist qualitative research responds to race, class, and gender inequality can inform future directions in qualitative inquiry. Black feminism as a theoretical framework and praxis is a useful and timely rejoinder to calls for more critical, relevant, action-oriented methodologies in social science research overall.

Black feminism is a useful lens for interrogating and analyzing racism, sexism, classism, homophobia, and xenophobia, while synchronously presenting an interposition to ideological segregation and bastardization that exists in the intellectual community. Such a covenant is achieved by including Black women as collaborators in qualitative research, drawing upon and referencing Black women theorists in scholarly writing, mentoring the next generation of critical race and Black feminist/womanist scholars, taking seriously the concerns that Black women and other people of color have about qualitative research, and exploring with a sense of urgency topics in qualitative inquiry that are of importance to Black women and other people of color. In closing, centering Black feminism in qualitative research facilitates critical understandings of how Black women creatively piece together their personal and shared realities into the qualitative research process and within and across cultural contexts. Much of our understandings of the social world are shaped by our experiences as daughters in an anti-Black and anti-girl world. *Daughtering* influences our approaches to data, theory, analysis, and representations of our observations and lived experiences.

FIELDNOTE 2

WITNESSES TO THE COVENANT

Sitting on my grandma's porch, getting my "hair did," I learned everything that I ever needed to know about being a girl on the south side of Chicago. See our lives back then were relegated to what existed between our legs and where we lived. Race was not an issue; everybody was Black, and affirmed, and celebrated.

Now, of course, other factors influenced our perceptions of ourselves, such as what block you lived on, who were your people, how light or dark was your skin, and how long was your hair. I had good hair. Long hair. Long thick, black hair. So, I spent a lot of time on the porch getting my hair did. All the master stylists on the block wanted to get their hands in my head. Or, maybe I wanted them to put their hands on my head. But, it was never for me to decide. My head was silently being auctioned off to the chosen one.

Back then, the women folk decided who was a reputable hair stylists—not some artificial license or the state; and mothers decided who was the best person to do their child's hair, based on the other woman's braiding skills (i.e. straight parts or sophisticated angles, thickness of braids or ponytails, angles, bead colors, oil and shine choices, etc.) and creativity (not too flamboyant, but definitely not boring), rela- tionship to the family, age, attitude, cost, friendliness, cleanliness, or some other unwritten rule. Oh, and she couldn't be too "heavy handed"! Being heavy handed is a deficit. The words, "She heavy handed" could kill one's dream of "doing hair."

Of course, your mama could do your hair, but you secretly wished for someone else to do your hair. Your mama (or anyone standing in her place for that matter) could hit you or chastise you verbally in front of everybody, if you became too squirmy or showed any discomfort. So, ideally, the young hip, cute Black girl would be chosen to do your hair. She wouldn't hit you, because she thought you were too sweet and cute. This girl was yet to have children of her own and we knew it. That's why she was our favorite. She still respected us and reserved some kind of empathy … at least until her own daughter came along, and she would become a designated mother of a girl child.

A girl child changes you. Birthing and raising a girl child toughens you up. Or, does simply becoming a mother on the south side toughen you up? Maybe the dude who left you with a baby changed you? Before the baby, she was strong and saw us—just as beautiful girls worthy of her time, compliments, and gentleness. Nevertheless, her temporary gentleness compared to our mothers' sternness was a momentary respite.

Anyway, no matter who did your hair, getting your hair did was not a private event, but a communal spectacle that took place in the kitchen or on the front porch. The artists needed to be able to see and talk to everybody. Maybe she needed to keep an eye on other children, gossip with other women, or get some fresh air, 'cause we know there was no air conditioning and all "dem' fans runnin', runnin' up da electric bill" as the grownups would say.

I liked the front porch best. If I couldn't play with my friends for hours, then at least I could watch others play. If they played really hard, then they couldn't see me wince and sweat from the pain. Or, was it torture?

Either way, mama and 'nem better never catch you making a face that indicated pain or anger. Period. If they did, the first thing that came out they mouf was, "What you frownin' fo?"

"It hurt."

"You know that don't hurt!" "You just tenda-headed."

Trust me, tender headed is the worst thing that you can be called as a Black girl on the block by a Black mother. Two things you don't want to be known for on the block are: tender headed or heavy handed. The designation "tenda-headed" is especially painful when everybody on the porch is listening and other girls are in earshot. By everybody on the porch, I mean, grown women. And grown women who mattered.

My grandmama's house, which was the family's house, was right in the middle of the block (and my godmama's house was only two houses down), placed me right in the center of grown folks' business when getting my hair done on the porch.

Children made the distinction early on between "grown folks' business" and everybody else's business, because the grown-ups would simply say when we asked a question or commented out of term, "Chile, you betta stay out of grown folk business."

On the porch, while getting our heads did, the grown folk just talked at us or over us. They knew we were listening, but they also trusted that we were the keeper of the secrets.

No matter what we heard come out of the grown folks' mouths, we knew not to repeat it. "Chir'ren" were taught early "not be tellin' my business." Not telling folks' personal or family business was a rule—not a written rule, but more like a moral code that if broken, if only once, could lead to your body parts coming in contact with any available foreign object, including a hair brush, house shoe, belt, hanger, or switch. Mama's or grandmama's hands were also quick and convenient weapons of choice.

Leaning back between your mama's legs, or someone's mama's legs (i.e. a grandmother, god mama, or play mama), with your head pushed forward, head tilted slightly to the left or the right, the girl child learned a lot of life's lessons by watching, (all the while pretending not to watch) and patiently listening.

We were not deaf or dumb, but good actors. Mimes?

Sitting on the porch getting our hair did, we were rarely directly talked to, unless we were told to do something. "Put the top back on that grease." "Go get the hairbrush." "Go get my pocket book." "Bring me my cigarettes." "You betta put yo' scarf on tonight."

On the porch, we learned our place in the world as girls/women and other girls/women's places in the world, based on another girl's/woman's place in the world, which was often unveiled based on other women's comments, judgments, and experiences; and the conversations us "chir'ren" were privy to or not privy to, omissions and admittances in conversations, verbal and non-verbal body language, laughter and sarcasm.

God forbid you ever got caught watching or listening.

"Girl, what you lookin' at?" or "Cover up your ears, chile" or "You bet not be tellin' my business" were all indicators that even when you heard or saw life through a Black woman's world, you better act like you did not hear or see nothing. In our interactions with other girls and women, in the middle of the block, on those front porches, sitting between a woman's warm black legs, we became witnesses to the covenant.

Fragmented realities

I was born on the south side of Chicago. My mother gave birth to me at Cook County hospital. A running joke that I have heard all my life is that this county hospital that serves the poor is a death ward. It kills more people than it saves. I was delivered early, and like most premature babies, I was underweight. I was 5 lbs. at birth. During family gatherings, I am reminded in loud and chuckling voices, "You were so tiny that your mama would put you in a dresser drawer to sleep, girl!" My birth story became a part of my identity—"I was always in a hurry. I been fast all my life. And, if I could thrive as a preemie and survive the Cook County hospital, I can survive anything."

At the age of 17, I was my mother's second born. My brother was one year and 25 days older than me. Coming along after me, not even a year later—10 months and 19 days—my sister was born. Even though we were born so close together, we functioned as three distinct personalities. My brother was high energy and athletic. Tall and skinny, to me, he seemed to be good at everything. He ran fast, jumped and climbed high, kicked and hit balls far. He was even really, really smart at school. My brother, or *Tam* his nickname, which we called him for short at home (because it was easier and quicker to say than his African name), even mustered up a good laugh from adults and our friends alike. Tam was good at everything that required smarts, including drawing, athletics, math, verbal communication, video games, etc.

Unfortunately, the one thing he was not good at was fighting. As a child, my brother was what kids in the neighborhood would call *a punk*. He was a dark reddish-brown boy, skinny, goofy, and smart living on Wood Street. That description alone made him an easy target for other boys who needed someone to take their frustrations out on and get their *street cred* up. Inevitably, his physical vulnerability required him to be mentally strong, but also a danger to himself and others. Due to my older brother's physical vulnerability in the concrete jungle, I was required to be physically and mentally strong.

On the other hand, my younger sister, Keke, who was born longer and heavier than me at birth (and has been taller than me ever since her first birthday), was meek and quiet throughout most of our childhood. She was a skinny child, yet heavier than me, with long lean legs, and kept a soft pretty smile on her face most times. She appeared always quiet and shy; too shy for her age. I can hardly remember my little sister speaking as a child. She mostly chose to speak to me, but rarely, if ever, spoke with strangers. Back then, I never thought she was handicapped or delayed compared to other children our age, but I certainly thought she put *me* at-risk in our neighborhood.

Her extreme shyness should have been a red flag to adults, but her extreme quietness (or mutedness) always went undetected. Unlike me and my brother, my sister was a real *yellow bone*. Or, what the grown folks called "hi yella" (as in high yellow). The grown folks say, "She was so yella, that when we took yo' picture, the flash would blind you; we couldn't see yo face in the picture; you was like the sun, shining in the picture!" Unlike me, Keke had nappy hair. The kind of hair mama and 'nem complained about when it was time to do it. Her kind of hair was referred to as a *mess*. "Girl, I don't feel like combing this mess."

Keke did not run, bike, or talk fast. But, she did learn fast, even if she was easily overlooked in a room. Maybe that is why she was mama's, grandmama's and auntie and 'nem's favorite. She was easy. She was also loving. "She would just curl up next to you like a cat," as auntie reminds us during flashbacks that are common during our family gatherings. In my memories, she was also easy for me. Easy to boss around and easy to be responsible for. I was the big sister who was always listened to and in charge of my sibling who was only one year younger than me, but light years behind me in attitude and mouth.

In Englewood (or whatever new community my young parents gravitated toward in their search for independence and adulthood), my sister made for easy prey around the neighborhood. She couldn't run or talk fast, which meant she needed to be a good fighter. She was certainly not a fighter; it was not a part of her natural disposition. Fortunately, she did not have to be, because I was a badass.

My mama taught us, "If one fight all fight," "If they beat yo ass, Im'ma beat yo ass," or "Don't let nobody put they hands on you!" Well, my sister (also known as baby girl) didn't seem to have a fight in her. She was not born that way, I thought. I thought she was weird. When a girl talk shit to her or hit her, my sister would just stare or cry. She was not a fighter. Eventually, I got tired of girls trying to pick on her, so I ran my mouth for her, and I took on all her battles, all the way through middle school. I also fought for or with my brother through his battles as needed as well. Nonetheless, city streets toughen everyone up eventually. My sister became a scrapper who fought her own battles (plus some) and my brother joined the ranks as a respected "G" (gangster) and drug dealer, not just on the block but them southside *streets*. Let's just say that nearly everybody at some point in my childhood or adolescent years became gang affiliated or gang active.

As for me, being the middle child, naturally my identity was constructed vis-à-vis my siblings (and who my daddy was or wasn't). Twenty days after my brother's first birthday, I was born. I was told that my father was not present at my birth. According to my mother's relatives, he was away in the military. According to my dad's relatives, I was loved from the beginning, if anything, too much by my dad's family. Apparently, my dad's family sent him away to the military to keep him out of trouble, which was too easy to find in Chicago's ghettos. He was known to smoke a little weed, sell drugs, indulge in alcohol, gang bang, and later affiliate with the Black Panthers.

Anyhow, if my brother's skin tone was reddish-brown, and my sister's sunshine-yellow, then my skin complexion was on the color scale between reddish dark brown and high yellow. Just brown, plain old brown. Nobody gave any attention to my skin color. And, if my brother and sister's hair were described as nappy (or having "beady-beads"), then my hair was "Indian hair." "She got that Indian hair from her daddy side."

Let the grown folk tell it, I got pretty much most of my features and characteristics from my daddy side. My big forehead, petite frame, short height, and talkin' tough (read: talkin' shit) came from my daddy side. Only a year behind my brother, I wanted to be my brother. So, naturally I do not recall what I was good at as a kid. He ran fast, but I did not run as fast as him, but I always wanted to be a fast runner. If he climbed trees and fences, then damnit, I would scale trees and fences. Since he was superb at math, then I needed to learn math. If he was the best at chess, spades, and Uno, then I needed to concentrate on how to outwit others around the table too. If he popped a wheelie on his bike while riding down the street, then I too was going to pop a wheelie, with or without a dress—it did not matter to me, as long as I was doing what he was doing.

But, in the real world, I was a girl; a tiny, underweight pretty girl. The boys didn't want to run against me, they wanted to kiss me, and later as a pre-adolescent, fuck me. Yes, where we were from, children were having sex or something resembling sex, and if one followed down the rabbit hole, soon enough it would be discovered that these sexually curious children were more than likely at some point some older teenager's or adult's prey. We never talked about such childhood sexual indiscretions though. Each child carried their own little secret it seemed.

Nevertheless, I couldn't be my brother, not simply because I was a girl, but because I was not him. My body was not equipped, and looking back, I obviously had some impulse control issues, according to today's science and education jargon. I talked a lot in class and out of turn; I cussed at other kids (like a sailor I might add) in the neighborhood, I beat up other girls and at times boys who thought they were tougher or more popular than me. At school, I didn't always complete homework, nor did I learn easily; however, I was still identified as gifted by the third grade. I was identified as gifted, because my brother was gifted; or did I work harder at school simply because my brother was studious and seemed to learn easily?

My mama never made a big deal out of school. It was common around the house to hear the grown-ups praise all three of us for how smart we were. In fact, as the grown-ups say, "I was mostly too smart for my own good," or "too grown for my own good," "And, ya'll smart like Peaches and Jerry."

My mama thought I was *fast*. "You so fast" and "Stop actin' fast" or "Imma beat yo' ass if you be out there actin' fast." My mama would describe me as fast. Not fast like my brother either, but *fast* in the sense of acting too much like an adult instead of staying in a child's place. I treated other children, especially my sister, like I was their mother. I wanted to boss other girls around or always be in charge of the situation. Even when grown women were around, I still treated the kids like they were my own kids—they were my responsibility. I told younger children how to behave, I organized and led playtime, and I disciplined and punished them when necessary.

My favorite games to play were "House" and "School," because I could tell the kids what to do, while sounding smart. Playing in the front yard, I would threaten the children and demand loudly with a mean face, "Sit yo' butt down or Im'ma tell mama," or when playing house, "I'm gon' whoop yo' butt, if you keep talkin'." I was being my mama even when mama, grandmama, auntie, or godmama were nearby.

By saying I was being too fast, the women folk were reminding me to just be a little girl. Stay in a child's place. I was a daughter acting like a mama. As a pre-teen, when I was not being "too fast" or "too grown," I was being described as a Tom-boy. "Stop acting like a Tom-boy!" Or "Stop being mannish!"

If being called *fast* was deprecating to a Black girl's ego, then being told not to act like a Tom-boy or "stop actin' mannish" was like snatching the life out of the Black girl's body. In an attempt to translate "acting fast," "acting like a Tom-boy," or "being mannish" much gets lost in the decontextualization of the phrases. All three phrases can be meant to celebrate a girl's risk-taking as well as warn her of the abnormality of her behavior and mannerisms.

For my mother(s), acting like a Tom-boy meant I was behaving in ways that only boys were meant and allowed to behave. Girls jumped Double-Dutch, for example, not popped wheelies on bicycles. Girls played hop-scotch, and did not attempt flips on abandoned mattresses left in empty lots. Girls sang songs, played hand games like "Twee-li—li," and we did not play "Hang-go-see" and "Cops and robbers" in gangways and alleys. Compared to being a Tom-boy, mannish was on a whole 'nother level. Being told to "stop acting mannish" was basically being told to stop acting like a man. Tom-boys broke gender rules, whereas mannish girls broke adult rules about gender roles.

I never wanted to be a man, but I certainly did not mind being a boy. Boys had more freedom. Girls never felt equal to boys in our expectations and desires, even though we were treated differently from our brothers. At times, we even made our own games up that our parents did not know about like "Catch-a-boy-kiss a boy," and as we aged, "Catch a boy-freak a boy." We were acting fast.

Nevertheless, I, like many Black girls, spent a lot of time navigating the liminal space between acting fast (i.e. acting like a woman) and acting like a Tom-boy (or mannish). We wanted to be good daughters. We yearned for the love and respect of the mothers around us. We wanted to become them, while simultaneously being respected, loved, and feared as they were by other mothers, the elderly, men folk, and other children in the community. But, we also wanted to be free, yet protected, on our own terms.

As for my mother, unlike sociological statistics would describe her, I never thought of my mother as a teenage mom, or single mom. She was simply mama. She behaved like every other mother and Black woman I knew. In the words of pop sensation Carl Carlton, my mother "was a bad mama jama," and when she walked down the street you would see her coming. She was "light-skin twin," and my uncle was "dark skin twin." She was popular in the neighborhood and everybody liked her.

Everybody called her by her nickname, "Peaches." I always called her "mama" or "ma," which got confusing at times, because when grandmama was around, we called her mama too. It wasn't until I was at my mama's funeral that I began to think about her birth name. Maybe I read it on the obituary or on all the government documents sent to me and my siblings—ward of the state papers, social security checks, birth certificates, or the death certificate.

Peaches mostly sported a curly moisturized fro. When she walked people noticed. She had big curvy hips, a big butt, and nice round boobs. She had big full lips, like mine, and chose to wear bright red lipstick or a dark brown glossy lipstick. Her lips were bold. My bold big lips made me a target for a lot of jokes in junior high and high school. Her lips simply got her a lot of attention. It was common for guys to acknowledge her body. "Hey, do fries come with that shake" is one memory I have of a man shouting at her as she walked down the street with us three. To this day, I wonder about how my mother felt about men's catcalls to her especially in the presence of three small children. I don't know if she liked the attention or not. She didn't pay them no mind.

See, when my mama walked, she "switched." She threw her ass and hips side-to-side hard. Real hard. In fact, I used to practice her switch around the house, and I think at some point, I perfected it, because grown-ups started telling me, "Stop switching with yo fast self!" And, as I got older, I would hear grandmama and them giggle and whisper to each other, "Look at her switching; walking like Peaches."

I did and do a lot of things like Peaches. My mother smoked, drank, and cursed like a sailor too. One of the fondest memories that I have of my mother is an image of her holding a set of cards in her hands, with a cigarette dangling from her lips, and her left eye half winked to keep the smoke out of her eye. I never took to smoking cigarettes (even though I tried puffing cigarettes a few times as a child, because that's what grown-ups do, right), but every now and again when I hit a joint, I let it dangle a little like mama.

My mother liked music and a good drink. Family rumor is that from the time I could walk, but before I could even talk, I would sneak and sip from my mother's drink. She preferred dark liquor, I believe Crown Royal, and she smoked Kools, but Salem could be a backup if the other brand was not available. My mother did not really go to church except for holidays like Easter Sunday. But, she did send my sister and me to church mostly with our godmothers or great aunts, and we attended vacation bible school every now and again in the summer.

But, she did claim a church home which I found out in 1982, when we attended her and my dad's marriage ceremony. By the time my parents were married, I was seven, my little sister six, and my older brother was eight years old. Reverend Hill, the man who baptized all three of us, officiated the wedding. Just a few hours before exchanging their vows, my mom and dad got into a heated argument that escalated quickly. My dad was fussing at her because she was still getting ready for the wedding, and he was angry that they were going to be late arriving at the church.

Like what happened often in our house between grown-ups, the argument began with yelling and cussing, and eventually turned into a physical fight. I cannot remember all the details, because kids did not listen to or watch grown-ups' arguments and fights. Besides, I was so nervous that I may have shut down emotionally. Over the years, I taught myself how not to show any emotions of fear. Despite pretending not to see and hear, I do recall my mother threatened not to go to the church with my dad.

I wanted the wedding to happen; I wanted them to get married. I was a daddy's girl. People actually called me "lil Jerry." I needed the wedding to happen to keep my daddy close and in the house with us.

Eventually, after everyone got cleaned up, all five of us (thank god), got in the car, and drove to the church. We were three hours late. The reverend conducted the ceremony and they exchanged vows in his office. Present were my parents, godmother, aunt, and uncle, and my siblings and me. There is no doubt that my dad loved my mom, but they stayed separated more than they stayed married in the first nine years of my life (oddly, she died two years after the ceremony, and only two months after another one of their separations). My mother was a tough Black woman to love or keep. If a man cussed at her, she would cuss back at him. And, if a man put his hands on her, or looked like he was going to put his hands on her, she kicked his ass.

My brother's father was not a part of our lives. If my memory serves me correctly, (and in my interpretations of court records), my brother's biological father was arrested for an armed robbery on the same day as my brother's first birthday. Since my brother was a New Year's baby, born on January 1st, I can only imagine that the crime he was arrested for was committed sometime between New Year's Eve and New Year's Day.

Also, I try to imagine what it must have been like for my mother as she celebrated her son's first birthday, prepared his first birthday party, and at the same time found out his dad could not be present. I can only imagine my mother feeling sad, disappointed, and embarrassed that her boyfriend never showed up, at her mother's house, to her first and only son's first birthday party, and her first birthday planned as a 16-year old mother. And pregnant with her second child. How did she survive the party and sleep that night?

My mother never displayed or voiced any animus toward my brother's father in front of us children. If anything, there was only a message of love and signs of flirtation between them, and even respect from his family for my mother. His family treated my sister and I like their own family; always showed love and provided us with good times and fun. As a family, my mother, with all three of us in tow, would take long trips to the prison where my brother's father was locked up, to visit him on visitation day. Those trips were a big deal.

All three of us children got dolled up for the trip. Mom packed the car with sandwiches for the long trip, and, yes, she got pretty. At the prison, in the southern part of Illinois, all the officers were White and men. The only woman was the officer who patted my mother down, and it looked from my innocent eyes like an arrest or public molestation. The White woman combed her fingers through my mom's hair, put her hand between her legs, and required her to open her mouth like a horse. My mother never looked at my sister and I when this happened, never commented on the treatment, or asked us how we felt about the pat down.

Shit, in retrospect, I didn't know if we were visiting the prison or checking into the prison. Nonetheless, the one or two prison visits to see my brother's father was like a field trip to see a distant relative. No one discussed it as fucked up or anything possibly devastating to young children's development. It was just another place where some adult Black men had to live. Without it being spoken, everybody just assumed it was more fucked up to leave a brother behind bars without receiving love and support from his family, or fucked up for children not to know or see their dads for long periods of time.

By the time I was an adult, I would visit another prison, a military prison, to visit my mother's twin brother. And years later, my own brother would find himself in prison as a young man despite his above average intelligence. Jails, prisons, and military service were not talked about at school, at church, or in books. Yet, these are places where many Black brothers, fathers, and uncles lived at some point in their life. Did our mothers' hearts remain locked up with them, while the other parts of their hearts waited patiently in government cheese lines until their return? Or, maybe they were too occupied raising the children to give attention to affairs of the heart? Meanwhile, the girl children watched the mothers ... in the kitchen, on the porch, in the parks, at church, and singing and dancing in the living rooms. As for the boy child? Maybe he just watched.

Reflective selves

Where I am from, women were accepted as strong and capable, and as nurturers and caregivers. In addition to being at the center of family and community life, they characteristically functioned interdependently. Collectively, in the kitchen, women and girls picked "the greens" off the stems, cleaned the chitterlings and greens, washed and dried the dishes collectively; women shared food stamps, stood in the food bank lines together in the early morning, and "watched" other people's children for free or in exchange for some of the collected food from the food bank; knocked door-to-door to help pay for the cost of a funeral, or together laid hands on someone to help relieve her suffering; and, because many of the women did not own cars or have a state issued driver's license, they transported each other back-and-forth for "a lil' gas money." In these moments is where we collectively witnessed and imparted rituals, norms, values, beliefs, and tradition.

Gendered cultural exchanges took place in the kitchen, on the front porch, on the back porch, in *laundry mats*, on park benches, or standing at the bus stop. The mothers were the heartbeat of the community—in fact, it was odd not to be a mother. Those who were not mothers were looked at *sideways*. The look on your mother's face or somebody's mother's face, or somebody's whispered overhead words, indicated that the non-mother was either "too fast" or a "tramp."

Even the *bulldaggers* had kids, back then. I believe I was nine the first (and last time), while sitting on the front porch with my friend, that I heard her mother describe another woman walking down the street, who looked and acted "mann-ish" as a *bulldagger*. They did not purposively use the term as a homophobic slur, but more as a description of character. Or, maybe they did use it as a slur. In that moment, a whole 'nother meaning was given to acting "mannish." She was an insider-outsider of the mother community.

Further, *holy* or sanctified women stood out as *non-birthers* (but that did not mean they were not mothers, in the cultural sense of the word). The community narratives that surrounded the holy women went something like after these women changed their once unholy ways as younger women, they simply could not find a decent church man to father a baby. Despite unspoken judgment, they were also revered in the community, because of their religiosity (i.e. discipline and obedience to the church) and willingness to nurture other people's children and serve the community, especially the elderly and sick. The holy women were eventually given a pass of judgment, because they became surrogate mothers for many others inside and outside of the neighborhood.

At any rate, even the late bloomers described above (including a few holy women) had children of their own sooner or later. Ironically, their babies usually arrived during hard times. Meaning, drugs, prostitution, jail, or some form of relationship violence surrounded narratives of the pregnancy and child's birth, which seemed like some kind of self-fulfilling prophecy predicted by the community mothers. These gendered narratives had damn near all of us born on the southside to a single parent mother at some point or another wondering about the story behind our own births and our mother's relationship with our fathers.

Despite a mother's circumstance, or maybe I should state, *in spite of the women around us set of circumstances*, interdependence functioned to make life easier for women, children, families, and all community members alike. We shared a set of circumstances that fostered a shared collective responsibility. Our collective consciousness more than likely was passed down by the generations from the continent of Africa and into the bellies of the slave ships, and to the slave quarters on southern slave plantations, and again up North during Black migrations. Our collective consciousness embraced interdependence as opposed to today's narrative of the independent Black woman stereotype. Instead, a collective consciousness was less about individual salvation or individual strength, and more about one's ability to mitigate and alleviate a shared burden, sort of speak.

Positioning the pieces

A woman's status was even more respected and valued if she was a good cook and homemaker (e.g. made sure her children were clean and obedient, took care of and respected the elderly, good at entertaining company, kept a clean and house, etc.). These well-rounded women—the good mothers, homemakers, and friendly—dominated a woman's place. Girls in our family took heed from other women and took, or were given, our rightful places sooner or later. Every woman knew her place in the family, which was situated somewhere between above the children, equal to men in mental and physical prowess, but positioned somewhere right below the status of man (i.e. husband, father, or boyfriend).

Even though a woman definitely would have a say and speak her mind during heated arguments or important conversations that required decision-making, men had the last say so on any topic. Moreover, daddies, boyfriends, and husbands made it known that they could throw their weight around if needed. At some point, in childhood, a child would hear a man threaten her mother, "You keep runnin' yo' mouth, Im'ma pop you in it." I rarely remember women who coiled under the threat of a man, and if she did, she was definitely determined as weak. Women were perfectly able to physically protect herself and her family, and it was accepted that she would do both as needed: with words or any other weapon, if necessary. Regardless of a woman's emotional or physical strength, being a man of the house was like holding the trump card. A woman knew when to shut up, speak up, or sit down; conversely, a man knew when and how to make a woman do as he wished. Once again, the girl child watched the women and the boy child watched.

Here is the contradictory world where Black girls lived and thrived—a world where we were recognized, needed, and strong, but our value always seemed to be juxtaposed to the boys and men around us. Black girls grew up with this juxtaposition in the back of our psyches. We took care of ourselves, we took care of younger children, served our fathers and elders first; and submitted to our mothers. There was actually a point in childhood where I came to believe that Black children, yes, specifically Black children (White children on television were always laughing and being loved and cared for by their parents), were put on Earth by god to be slaves to their parents.

By the age of five, we were told "Be a big girl." Being a big girl meant walking to the corner store to buy something for the house, "and make sure you hold your sister hand when crossing the street." Being a big girl required you to be sure the men in the house were served their dinner plate first, and the first or last piece of meat. We answered, "Ma'am?" "Yes, ma'am, no ma'am," to our mothers and grandmothers. Personally, I did not mind humbling myself before the elder for they at least showed gratitude and noted, "What a sweetheart you are, baby. You didn't have to do that."

Big girls cooked and cleaned not only our rooms, but the kitchen, living rooms, family rooms, and bathrooms. Big girls also washed, folded, and ironed clothes. We also bathed babies and helped younger siblings with school work. It is no wonder, then, that by the time I was 14, I would think to myself or write in my journal "I'm 14, but I feel like I'm 40."

Some of my fondest memories are of me helping my sister study the state capitals, quiz her on the constitution, drill her the multiple tables for math, and listen to her practice the clarinet (absolute torture). Inside the house was the women and girls' workspace. Outside the house the boys and men cut grass, hauled trash to the corner, or painted the exterior of the house when needed. Us girls, we only worked outside to plant seasonal flowers, sweep the yard, or pull weeds.

Being a big girl prepared us to be good wives, students, and caregivers I suppose. All the while we existed within a family structure and community that judged us on how well we did all the aforementioned. Growing up, I had little cares about how White people viewed me, because I was overly concerned with how other Black women and men received my presence. Was I pretty and respectable enough? Was I able to care for children and the elderly? Was I smart enough and strong enough? A girl's internal ruminations on these questions and her unmediated responses could either educe feelings of positive self-worth or damage a positive sense of self.

As for me, I rebelled in my early adolescent years. The truth was, at least in my mind, I was too skinny and petite to live up to Black standards of beauty. My body frame simply did not bless me with a big ass, wide hips, large breasts, or round thick thighs. Even more, the "good girl" message did not work for me, because I did not like the idea of being expected to bear children. I could not stand the thought of being a mother!

Somewhere between childhood and adolescence, mothering became a chore and being a woman a heavy burden to bear. I did not enjoy cooking or even touching raw meat (e.g. pork chops, chicken, ham, or turkey); and I thought men were lazy and women were stupid and weak for taking care of them. By the time high school rolled around, my elders determined that I was ruined for marriage. I hated everything domestic and made it well known verbally. Needless to say, I got cussed out or got my ass beat a few times for my rebellious ways.

In fact, the hardest smack I ever received is when I mumbled under my breath while washing dishes at the family's kitchen sink, "Why don't the boys have to wash dishes and cook?"

Standing next to me, my auntie swiftly responded in a matter of fact manner, "My mama didn't make my brothers do no cooking and cleaning." Her retort sounded to me like an excuse, as if it was just like this because this is how it has always been for us girls and she too was a victim. Trust me, my sister and I heard this excuse before when we questioned the order of things.

Before I knew it, being sassy and ready for a fight, I retorted, "That's why they lazy and keep going to jail and living with grandmama, because she never made them do nothing. The same thing gon' happen to the boys."

My auntie smacked the taste out of my mouth! I ain't even see it coming. I stood there stunned and speechless with my face on fire. I knew I had crossed the line. My brother and cousins were "the boys." I spoke out loud every Black mother's worst fear, and simultaneously, verbalized the silenced dialogue in the Black family.

Binding contested memories

Soon enough, the family accepted that I was not going to force fit myself into some small airtight, but absolutely fragile, box of Black womanhood. They began to plant ideas about education and careers in my head, for they surmised that there was no way a good man was going to take care of me and tolerate my non-domestic and Tom-boyish ways. Naturally, "You would make a good lawyer, because you like to argue and talk back."

At some point, I did decide that I would become a lawyer, but only to become the first woman president. Olive Oyl, Popeye's girlfriend, convinced me when she sang, "If I was president ..." that I too could become the president of the U.S. For the record, I never got the memo that there had never been a Black person president. As a young girl, Olive Oyl and Wonder Woman were my women superhero role models. Can you think of any Black women or girl cartoon characters on television in the late 1970s and 1980s? Every girl desired to become what she saw TV in the kitchen, or on the block, right?

By high school, I had been introduced to the civil rights movement and Black nationalism from within my family and popular culture. In retrospect, I now know that the elders began to read my rebellious spirit and intentionally fed into my appetite for anti-authority and counterculture. Not only did elders share stories of their own participation or support of the movement, but they also openly discussed what they appreciated about the movement and what strategies they did not think worked in the best interest of Black people. They went even further in their explanations with active young listeners and discussed what more needed to be done politically and culturally on behalf of Black people.

For instance, my maternal grandmother embraced the initiatives of the Black Panthers, and she was a grassroots activist in Chicago. She advocated for access to free and affordable housing for the homeless on Chicago's south side. Grandma (or mama as we called her), and the organization group she was a part of, could not understand why the city of Chicago would allow abandoned houses to accumulate in Black neighborhoods and arrest transients who sought shelter in those houses. The organization pushed for city government to fix up abandoned houses and empty lots, and make the houses suitable safe shelters or affordable housing for the poor.

One of the bravest memories that I have of my grandmother is of her saving a young woman's life. In short, we were awakened in the middle of the night to screaming sounds of a woman. Our neighbor, who lived in the lower part of the family house, once again was beating his wife. We were all awakened in the middle of the night to her screams. The police were called and so was my grand-mother. I do not know who called, but both arrived at the same time. Come to find out, the neighbor, a Vietnam veteran, attempted to literally "iron" his wife. My grandmother touted her gun in the air, and demanded over and over again, "Muthafucka get out my house! Get out my house! Get yo' shit out my house and don't come back!"

In my eyes, grandma, who a few years later became my legal guardian after my mother's untimely death, was a brave and bold superhero. The Vietnam vet, who I cannot for the life of me recall his name, left and never came back to the house. Later on the same night that he was kicked out the family house, I revealed to my grandmother and mother that he had molested me several times in the middle of the night. I usually woke up to him touching me, even though I learned to feign sleep. Is it possible for a child to *feign sleep*? Did he touch my sister and brother too? Yes, we all shared a bedroom until around the age of nine. How many times had he visited our bedroom? I will never know, because when you are a child, sleep bends and morphs time (or is it trauma bends and morphs time?).

Living on the *other side* of the tracks, my paternal grandfather also influenced my identity politics. As I came into my political consciousness in middle school, my grandfather began to share more explicitly stories of my aunt, my father's sister. Apparently, I was a "spittin' image" of my aunt, in stature, skin complexion, rebellion against traditional gender roles, and speaking unapologetically about "race" and "my people." Even when my daddy was dismissing me as "crazy," my grandfather took my curiosity about Black liberation seriously. Thus, my grandfather fed my curiosity through stories and pictures.

According to my grandfather, he sent my aunt away to college, and she became active in the Black Panthers Party against his sentiments. He showed me pictures of my aunt on his wall sporting big afros and black leather jackets. I think secretly he revered her sophistication, aesthetics, and steadfast dedication to the movement. However, as he explained to me, once she began talking about "Back to Africa" politics, he became even more disenchanted with her newfound stance on racial apartheid in the U.S. He was a Korean war veteran who chose different means to address White supremacy and racial inequality. He preferred the teachings of Christianity, Dr. Martin L. King, and peaceful protest. For granddaddy, education, voting, and peaceful protest were the path to Black liberation. I believe he thought that I was more like my aunt, and he came to embrace my politics and was my main supporter.

Peculiarly, my uncle, my mother's brother, introduced the family to Afrocentrism and Pan Africanism in the late 1980s. In the mid-1980s, just a year or two after my mother's death, my uncle moved into my grandmother's home. Family rumor suggests he fell on hard times after Vietnam, and she could protect (economically) and help care for him (mentally) as he got back on his feet. As he shared with me, after Vietnam, he turned to drinking. To stop drinking alcohol, he turned to Rastafarianism to save his life. Many of our family gatherings, reunions, celebrations, memorials centered Africa, Rastafarianism, Black liberation, Black nationalism, Black spirituality, ancestral callings, etc.

In reflection, those gatherings were deliberate attempts to acknowledge, grasp, and pass down African and Black American culture. As a teenager, the gatherings and rituals alike made me feel different, or maybe, even exotic or extreme in the eyes of my peers. I did not have the forethought or think to care at the time how much those family and communal rituals would later impact my thinking about the social world and how to go about changing it. Serendipitously, at the same time that my uncle was conscientiously attempting to instill African-centered culture into the family's youth, my generation of ghettozied youth were in the midst of a cultural revolution.

We yearned for a war cry. We yearned for something to explain to us why everything around us seem to be falling apart. Families were breaking up, mothers were on crack, brothers were in jail, fathers were absent. The police were White. Teachers were White. Social workers were White. Doctors were White. Television was White. To me, as a young girl surviving on the block, hip hop and rap represented both my rage and my celebration of life. As a matter of fact, it was also hip hop that further got me interested in Black women's empowerment and Black empowerment. Black women's creativity, bodies, and independence were being celebrated alongside calls for a Black consciousness.

Queen Latifah, adorned in African attire, called for the unity of Black men and women and MC Lyte reported in rhyme that she was as "hard as a rock or I should say a boulder." At the same time, KRS-1 reminded myself and peers that "we were headed for self-destruction," if we did not become more conscious of the damage that White supremacy institutions posed. Accordingly, Public Enemy suggested we needed to "fight the power" and warned us of cultural appropriation and hegemony as well as the urgent need for self-awareness. Even more radical, NWA sent the message via the underground railroad (i.e. underground rap) not to trust the police and speak boldly against state sanctioned violence.

Truth be told, I learned of most of these rap artists through my brother and cousin. Rap music was not welcomed openly in our home. For my aunt and uncle (who my siblings and I resided with full-time after my mother's death), rap music was too vulgar and violent, so the boys played it in their rooms or watched the videos on MTV and BET, when our parents were not present. As is well known, back then and now, in hip hop, we witnessed, and continue to encounter, images of despair, degradation of women, and disparaging images of the Black community, alongside celebrations of violence and drug and gang culture.

As expected, rather than our parents accepting hip hop culture, they preferred R&B (Rhythm and Blues). They blared Luther Vandross, Gerald Levert, Anita Baker, and the Isley Brothers through the living room speakers. Personally, I can admit that together hip hop and R&B shaped my personality. R&B appealed to my budding adolescent sensuality while hip hop helped me claim my right to *express* my sexuality as a liberated girl/woman. Janet Jackson, Whitney Houston, Tina Turner, and Karyn White (and let's not forget Madonna and Cindy Lauper) reminded me that being a young woman with emotions and desires was normal. Meanwhile, hip hop reminded me that I was in opposition to ...

As an adolescent with an impressionable mind, I clung to an unwavering message of women's right to freedom of expression alongside a Black liberation agenda. In my mind, while both young men and women both rapped for Black rights and power, Black women were the only ones who rapped to beats about Black women's esteem. Although many rappers openly paid homage to Black women in their lyrics, in particular their mothers or a young woman's physique, even the most race conscious rappers failed to address gender oppression within the Black family and community. KRS-One's 1993 album, "Brown Skin Woman," actually pointed out the misogyny and hypocrisy in hip hop culture.

Inexplicably, many well-known Black women rappers' lyrics creatively and sophisticatedly cogitated on misogyny, affirmation of Black men and women, cultural pride, and racial liberation. These two seamless ideologies in hip hop culture, a *Black (masculine-centered) liberatory* imagination and a *women's cultural standpoint*, along with familial socialization, meshed together to encode my approaches to self-expression and an embodied politic. For girls like me, the White man's created ghettos not only put us in danger inside our own homes, but they also became spaces of sexual and racial terror.

Conspicuously, at the same time that young people were on the airwaves pushing back against White dominance, and asserting women's right to self-determination, the U.S. government had waged a war on drugs and poverty. This war had become many of my family members', neighbors', and classmates' daily reality. As daughters, we were being reared to fight in and survive this war (against our humanity); *daughtering* (conscious and subconscious performances) became our internalized coping mechanism during times of war.

As hinted at above, the elders had somewhat warned and prepared me, and others of my generation, of such a proverbial war. Fortunately, due to the multitude of diverse images, life histories, and familial and cultural teachings that had been overtly and covertly impressed onto my psyche, I learned to concomitantly identify Black vulnerability/pain, resistance, and power in all of its multifacetedness and subversive-ness. This tripartite became my matrix for excavating Black girls' and women's unconscious ideas, feelings, and cultural expressions while also confronting the rhetoric and mythos of science.

FIELDNOTE 3

DECOLONIZING THE MIND

Most of the contributions to Black feminist anthropology are explicit about how their present-day thinking was forged out of a tradition of Black American resistance rooted in the politics, praxis, and poetics of runaway slaves, slave rebellions, Maroons, the underground railroad, slave narratives, Negro spirituals, anti-lynching campaigns, the Civil Rights movement, black organizations, the Black nationalist movement, the Black aesthetic, and most recently, reggae and consciousness hip-hop.

~ Irma McClaurin (2001, p. 4)

Exhibit A: Dr. Venus E. Evans-Winters for BlackAdemics. KLRTV-PBS, Texas. February 17, 2018

Racialized Terror: Trauma Inside and Outside of Schools

Can I keep it real for a moment?

Adverse childhood experiences: Stressful or traumatic events with potentially negative lasting effects on health and well-being.

For Black children, "Adverse Childhood Experiences," go way back!

For Black children, "stress and traumatic events" go back to the Transatlantic Slave Trade, chattel slavery, sharecropping, southern lynch laws and Jim Crow Laws, and the racial terror Black children suffered when they engaged in efforts to desegregate public schools.

For Black children, "stress and trauma" looks like eugenic policies in schools that labeled Black children as mentally retarded, learning disabled, and behaviorally-emotionally disturbed for decades following Brown vs. Board of Education and the Nation at Risk report.

Today, I want to have a FOR REAL conversation about trauma.

Let's just say that I know a little something about trauma; not simply as a mental health professional and educator, but also because I survived the 1990s. Chicago born and Southside Bred.

My friends and I spent our teen years, and, came into young adulthood in the 1990s. Admittedly, the 1990s were fun times for my peers and me.

We had Michael Jackson, Janet Jackson, Whitney Houston, and Tupac; MC Lyte, Queen Latifah, Nas, NWA, X Clan, KRS-1, Anita Baker and the almighty Queen Lauryn Hill!

Beyond the obvious contradictory adolescent 1990 messages of love and lust, racial and gender pride, my generation was also coping hard with the WAR on drugs (or shall I say Black bodies).

We observed first hand our families and neighborhoods destroyed by 1990s drug sweeps, mass policing and knock-knock policies. You know what knock-knock means?

"Knock-knock," then the police knock your doors down and enter your house or your neighbors' house with military style weapons.

It was like the people who we were taught were supposed to be there to protect us, were the same people in uniforms who decided overnight, while we were sleeping, to wage terror on our homes, Black boys and men, and our neighborhoods.

Police sirens were our alarm clocks between 12am and 5am. I guess the children in my neighborhood didn't need or deserve sleep. To this day, I still sleep lightly at night awakened by any footsteps or a "knock-knock."

Sadly, in that short but seemingly drawn out decade, I personally witnessed police drug raids, neighborhood sweeps, gang shootouts on the block; and the loud weeps and screeches of mothers, girlfriends, and grandmothers as they stood over the coffins of their teen boys and young men; unlike myself who had no tears to shed at my own brother's funeral, because dying young was the new black for my generation.

So, yes, I (like many who survived the 90s) know trauma beyond books and theories and other people's stories.

In fact, the majority of us, who come from where I come from, not only survived but we thrived, and we are now raising children of our own.

Recently we are being triggered, because we are not only witnessing new forms of domestic terror, but also the residual effects of the War on Drugs and mass incarceration through our children's eyes this time.

My own son, for example, is 17, and a senior in high school.

In his short lifetime, he has already lived through numerous acts of mass violence on U.S. soil, including 9/11, Columbine, Sandy Hook, Virginia Tech, the Orlando Night Club and Las Vegas music festival shootings. And, as of this week, the Florida school shootings.

Obviously, as a mother, I want to protect all children from being exposed to any acts of violence; however, as a Black mother, I am particularly concerned with the direct and indirect racial violence Black children are exposed to consistently.

My son and the youth I serve have had to cope with the very public killings and mournings of: Trayvon Martin, Jordan Davis, Rekia Boyd, Michael Brown, Eric Garner, Laquan McDonald, Tamir Rice, Freddie Gray, Sandra Bland, and Korryn Gaines.

However, racialized trauma does not only occur on highways and street corners.

Systematic violence, such as policing in schools, harsh discipline and zero tolerance policies, further threaten the psychological well-being of Black children.

Far too many of our schools are reminiscent of prisons and mental health wards. As one teenage girl told me, "Teachers treat us just like we in jail, Dr. V!"

Are schools driving our boys and girls crazy or pushing them into prisons?! It is a fair question to ask.

Today, I draw upon the example of my son's childhood, reflections of the youth I serve, and my own adolescent years to demonstrate that trauma in the lives of many Black children is actually generational trauma linked to structural violence and racialized policies inside and outside of schools.

Racialized policies over the last few decades look like disinvestment in: public education, affordable housing, reproductive health care, mental health, and recreational services in Black communities.

Structural violence looks like: lack of access to clean water, nutritional foods, jobs with a living wage, and of course, fear of police violence and acts of racial terror.

I have to raise the uncomfortable question: "How do we meet the needs of students in our schools who are coping with generational racialized trauma?"

This simple question reframes the cause of trauma and locates the problem within our systems and institutions, and not solely within individuals, families, or certain student groups.

This simple rephrasing emphasizes that children are not broken, deficient, or pathological; the reality is that our nation's institutions, including many of our school systems, are broken and plagued with the diseases of racism and classism.

See, Ida B Wells, Marcus Garvey, Carter G Woodson, Malcolm X, Mary McCleod Bethune, Septima P Clark, Gwendolyn Brooks, John Henry Clarke, and Asa Hilliard to name a few, were all Black intellectuals and cultural workers who predicted the psychological assault that racism and White supremacy would inflict on the psyche of the Black child and family.

Moreover, beyond mere predictions, all of the aforementioned scholars also proposed the type of education that would be needed to develop and sustain the socio-emotional and cultural health of Black children and adults.

In other words, discussions on the effects of trauma on the growth and development of Black children are nothing new. What is new, however, are those who are attempting to "treat" and "diagnose."

With all due respect, schools are not triage centers nor are teachers mental health professionals.

Thus, truly trauma informed schools will take the bold move to embrace a cultural framework to address racialized trauma.

In the words, of the great Lauryn Hill, "How you gon win, if you ain't right within?"

Right now, many of our systems, including schools, are not "right within." Therefore,

First, we call for racialized trauma interventions that serve to acknowledge and mediate historical and contemporary patterns of economic oppression and exploitation, housing discrimination, political disenfranchisement, and education inequality.

Second, our children need access to Black teachers and Black mental health professionals who are sensitive and knowledgeable about the cultural, intellectual, and emotional needs of Black children and families.

Thirdly, as our ancestors once pointed out and current Black scholars contend, there is a need for curriculum that centers and affirms the identities, histories, and experiences of the Black child and other Africans across the Diaspora.

Lastly, we call for a moratorium on exclusionary school practices with the intention to disrupt the school-to-prison pipeline. A moratorium on school expulsions should stay in effect until racial disparities in school discipline is eliminated within and across districts.

In closing, racialized trauma is real and killing many of our children softly, but surely. It will take all of us to help heal and rebuild the spiritual and cultural wealth of our youth, so that one day they can call upon their ancestral knowledge to help lead and heal this nation.

Ashe'!

Magical realism

One of the biggest myths feeding the psyches of educators is that young Black people enter classrooms and the learning process as blank slates. In the U.S., we are socialized to perceive Black people as morally, intellectually, physically, culturally, and aesthetically inferior to White people. Media, religion, schooling, parental upbringing, peer relationships, etc., teach White people that Black people are naturally inferior and that White people are rightfully superior. Consequently, the average teacher views Black students as inherently *deficient*, lacking of purpose, and in need of mending. Informed by so-called objective science, education systems perpetuate racialized myths of inherited deficiency.

Erasure discourse

A few common phrases used to describe students at all levels of education are: *at-risk students, urban students, high needs students, Title I students, diversity students, first generation college students*. At some point in my own academic socialization or work in schools, I have heard school administrators, teachers, or board members use any one of these phrases to describe their mostly Black student population. Exactly, who are at-risk students? Are not all children and adolescents *at-risk* of emotional, physical, medical, or academic stressors that is by virtue of being a human child during a vulnerable stage of development? Similarly, all children have *high needs* and teachers should be prepared to meet students diverse needs.

Likewise, the concept *diverse students* makes no sense from a developmental standpoint. Quite frankly, humans are, scientifically speaking, biologically (or is it physiologically?) and phenotypically diverse. So, who exactly are the *diverse students* on any given campus? How are schools defining *urban* students, considering that the term urban is a social construction with different meanings in different contexts? How are suburban students different from *urban* students? As for *Title I students*, it is an educational policy, so how does a child or group of students become a *policy*? Such deficit-oriented language exposes deficit-thinking in education.

Moreover, these categorizations objectify and dehumanize the very children for whom civil rights activists have struggled to get school actors to recognize their humanity for centuries. The problem of inequity in the nation's educational system becomes situated within the child (and racial or social group) as opposed to decades of systematic exclusion and marginalization of certain student groups. And, lastly, the most egregious and telling phrase used in higher education today is the term *first generation students*. Even many students of color refer to themselves as *first generation students* or a *first generation college student*. It is common for the oppressed to take on the language of the oppressor.

However, as I have illustrated throughout this book, Black students and other students of color enter classrooms, colleges, and universities carrying the cultural legacy and knowledge of generations. Some students may be the first in their family to physically step foot on a college campus, or they are the *first in their family to attend college*, but that does not mean it is their first time learning; or that their appetite for learning or studying different cultures suddenly started when they entered that college space. This language, like all racialized language, erases students' culture and humanity.

Language is political and can serve both a functional (i.e. a word or phrase is more efficient for a sound bite) and psychological purpose. In this case, a simple term can wipe out an entire generation of people. For instance, Black people have been in North America for at least 400 years, and have been the longest living, exploring, inventing human species on the planet. Therefore, it becomes oxymoronic to refer to any Black person with African ancestry as *first generation*. Politically, all of the aforementioned euphemisms are a threat to the psychology of the Black student, and latently propagates a White superiority complex.

Many of the racialized myths about Black inferiority entered schools off the back of the Eugenics movement (early 1900s–1960s) and were solidified with the 1965 *Moynihan Report*. Whereas Eugenics science embedded in curriculum and educational theory that Black people were inherently lazy, feeble-minded, and unattractive, the *Moynihan Report* convinced the public and policymakers that the Black family was incapable of meeting the emotional and educational needs of the youth. Based on this report, education policymakers and teacher education programs set out to bring structure and discipline, a work ethic, and moral character to countless Black children in *urban ghettos*. By the 1970s and 1980s, teachers became determined (or maybe mandated) to deliver students like me from destitution and into salvation.

Today's educators advocate for curriculum that addresses *adverse childhood experiences* (ACE), *socioemotional learning* (SEL), and character and moral education. In countless schools serving culturally and linguistically diverse students, educators are becoming pseudo-psychologists and spiritual leaders calling for mindfulness practices and meditation in the classroom. At the other end of this spectrum are educators who demand students be *resilient*, and that we let them fail, so that they can develop *grit*. To clarify, these psychoeducational theories and approaches themselves are not wholly malapropos. However, I contend that most of these approaches have (1) become mechanisms for the *informal* diagnosis and treatment of Black students, (2) serve to *fix* the student as opposed to confront socio–economic inequality and racial hierarchies in society, and (3) force students of various racial, ethnic, linguistic, and social class backgrounds to conform to White middle-class culture in schools.

Deficiency discourse

Notwithstanding the obvious scapegoating of poor working-class families and students of color, which is consistent with racist thinking in this country, the focus on the so-called internal deficits and moral aptitude of Black students is consistent with Eugenics science in education. Discourse of deficiency and pathology simply has become a part of the popular imagination. The consequence is that when Black students enter schools and universities the assumption is that (a) the curriculum will offer us everything that we need to know, (b) we do not have any ambitions of our own as it relates to knowledge/truth seeking, and (c) the intellectual and cultural predilections of the Black students are the very same as that of White students.

To the contrary, younger Black people enter formal education environments with acquired tastes, beliefs, habits of mind, and understandings of the social world, all of which are informed by our upbringing within our families and communities. We do not enter the classroom as culturally deficient or as empty vessels. For me, it was right around the fifth grade that I began to conscientiously merge myself into the knowledge making and understanding process. Outside of school, my parents primarily taught math and reading through games and organized play. Double-dutch, dominoes, spades, solitaire, Uno, *I Declare War*, and *Rummy 500* indirectly taught us math skills, like prediction and calculation; and brain teaser and logic games books that my mom and dad purchased served to build our critical thinking skills and problem-solving skills.

Meanwhile, the Black History Month television showings of the Dr. Martin L. King documentary and the TV series Roots were required annual viewing to teach us our history, and Sunday morning gospel music kept us spiritually awakened at home. In our all Black schools in Chicago, in the early 1980s, we still sang the Negro National Anthem after recitation of the Pledge of Allegiance.

Admittedly, it was not until my family moved to a collar south suburb of Chicago, in 1984, that race became an obvious factor in life. Just walking to school became a safety issue for us. We were taught early not to walk to school alone since White people actively harassed us to and from school, to and from the park, to and from sporting activities. Racists were bold and loud, shouting "Niggers, go back to Africa!" Some White neighbors placed signs in their windows that read "Hell no, we want go." Those signs indicated that Black people would not move into their neighborhoods or push White homeowners out the neighborhood without a fight.

We were naive children back then, because race/racism was not at the center of our universe, being a child and enjoying parks, community swimming pools, and open space to run about brought us joy. We were blinded by the physical openness and pristine of suburban space. Openness and pristine could not be used to describe our neighbors. One time my sister selling Girl Scouts' cookies knocked on the front door of a house that was located on the "Blacks are not welcomed" side of town.

We adventured out to that side of the neighborhood, because we wanted a selling advantage and thought we could increase our profits. But, after my sister knocked on the door, a faceless woman yelled, "Honey, there's a nigger at the door!" My sister and I took off running without looking back.

On another occasion, we were caught off guard again, as we cracked jokes and giggled while we walked home from the neighborhood park. A loud engine revved, and we looked up, and a young White man spit chewed up chips in my sister's face and spouted, "Nigger, go back to Africa!" My return tort was, "Honky, go back to Europe!" I spent the next few blocks regretting that I failed to protect my fragile little sister. I should have known better to walk so openly on the sidewalk.

Us Black girls experienced these *minor* assaults, but the boys experienced more aggressive or direct confrontations and encounters with White citizens and White authorities, including police and fire department officials. As minors, the boys were called niggers, verbally assaulted, roughed up, chased and arrested or escorted home by the police for minor infractions like curfew violation, trespassing, and insubordination.

Invisible/hypervisible

Fortunately, my parents were vigilant and did the best that they could to protect us and push back against racial harassment. However, as the young men in the neighborhood aged, the violations and arrests became more serious (e.g. traffic violations, overnight jail stays, and court fines). Within a couple of years of our parents' purchasing our home, in that small working–class suburb where most people worked in factories or with the railroad, White flight happened overnight. Inside of our neighborhood school, I certainly had my battles at school, but school was a site of refuge. I enjoyed the learning process, but despised schooling.

I have discussed elsewhere my schooling experiences in a segregated suburb (Evans–Winters, 2005), so here I want to give attention to the development of my emancipatory consciousness. At school, teachers, libraries, and books were entry points to worlds beyond my reality, including other people's worlds, personalities, and histories that would become my blueprint for a critical consciousness.

It was early in middle school when books became my chosen medium for travel to other times and places. If members of my family communicated the quest for Black power, and hip hop painted a magical portrait of oppression and struggle (as a contemporary and futuristic manifestation), then it was books that granted me the opportunity to travel to different historical and cultural contexts in search of a different way of life. Oddly enough, there is not one teacher in middle school that I can point out as my favorite.

Even when teachers treated me well as a student, there was always a White student nearby who was treated better or given more attention. Also, on the surface, we did not have much in common culturally with our all White teaching staff. In those days, there were not conversations about multiculturalism or culturally responsive teaching; teachers taught and students were expected to learn. I always sensed that we were burdens to those teachers.

At times, I felt sorry for the teachers, because some of the Black students were out-right rude and disrespectful to the White teachers, such disrespect was not present at my all Black school in the city. In the all Black city schools, we would have been paddled at school by the teacher, or whooped when we got home by our parents. White teachers at my new suburban elementary school were passive. Or, were they simply passive aggressive? In Chicago schools, I always felt pushed to be above average or toward excellence by our Black teachers.

In reflection, in our suburban school with those White teachers, we were simply being schooled. Teachers were, in essence, passive toward our education. But, one teacher, Mrs. Fahey, in sixth grade accidentally (or intentionally?) planted the seed that helped to cultivate a critical race consciousness when she discovered I was an avid reader.

Exhibit B: Books that fostered a critical race gender imagination by stages

Her eyes were watching God

In early adolescence, books with an adventurous girl character at the center of the narrative intrigued me the most. Obviously, there were not many books with girl characters as heroines when I was growing up, and there certainly were not many books with a Black girl character in the storyline. Therefore, it was a welcome surprise when Ms. Fahey assigned me the book *Roll of Thunder, Hear My Cry* by Mildred Taylor (1976). In hindsight, White girl characters, like Romano Quimby and Margaret, momentarily offered me access to adventures in safer worlds where periods and private talks with God did not automatically make you fragile or peculiar.

Conversely, the Black girl narrator, Cassie Logan, in Taylor's book illustrated for Black youth readers the values and morals pivotal to exist safely and righteously in a White supremacist society. Racial pride and dignity were at the center of the

Middle School	High School	Undergraduate
Roll of Thunder Hear My Cry (Mildred Taylor)	I Know Why the Caged Birds Sing (Maya Angelou)	Feminist Theory: From Margin to Center (bell hooks)
Are You There God, It's Me, Margaret (Judy Blume)	The Heart of A Woman (Maya Angelou)	The Isis Papers (Frances Cress-Wesling)
Romano Quimby, Age 8 (Beverly Clearly)	Malcolm X Autobiography	Native Son & Black Boy (Richard Wright)
Part of My Soul Went With Him (Winnie Mandela)	Tar Baby (Toni Morrison)	No Disrespect (Sister Souljah)
Sula (Toni Morrison)	Little Women (Louisa May Alcott)	Invisible Man (Ralph Ellison)
Song of Solomon (Toni Morrison)	Their Eyes Were Watching God (Zora Neale Hurston)	Making Face, Making Soul (Gloria Anzaldua)
Kaffir Boy (Mark Mathabane)		Our Nig (Harriet E. Wilson)
Temple of My Familiar (Alice Walker)		The Bond's Woman Narrative (Hannah Crafts)

narrative of the Black girl odyssey. After reading *Roll of Thunder, Hear My Cry*, I searched out for other books that intersected race with gender and location.

Curiously, I found Toni Morrison's books *Sula* (1973) and *Song of Solomon* (1977) on the bookshelf in my family home, next to the full set of Britannica Encyclopedias that were sold to my parents by a White door-to-door salesman. Due to our parents' constant reminders, and insistence on us using the heavy ass encyclopedias for research and class projects, we knew that the encyclopedias were expensive and bought on credit. Anyhow, it was common for me to grab a book off the shelf randomly, or at the request of my aunt. In our house, if someone said that they were bored, our parents would retort, "You bored? Read a book!"

My mind did not require boredom to read, I simply read and researched (flipping through the Britannica books for random facts and images) at will. I would constantly ask for permission to walk for miles and cross over into White territory to get to the public library. When the public library or school library was not an option, then I would pull a book off the bookshelf in the family room. To this day, I cannot help but wonder if *Sula* and *Song of Solomon* were age-appropriate.

However, the women characters and themes raised in both texts questioned the taken for granted (i.e. marriage, childbirth, segregation and environmental racism, and mental illness) and the taboo (i.e. rape, same gender intimacy, interracial relationships, family abandonment, etc.). As a literary genius, Toni Morrison magically illustrated how Black people's lives were constantly being challenged and shaped by White people's desires, needs, and fears, and, simultaneously, hindered by Black men's emotions and dreams. Interestingly enough, the women characters in Morrison's and Taylor's books were asking similar questions about girls' and women's relationship to the spiritual and physical realm.

For many Black girls and women characters, they continuously contemplated how to transcend the physical realm to escape the weight of racism, poverty, loss and abandonment. Black women, young and old, embraced each other and the spiritual realm for together they represented hope. What is the purpose of living and loving in a hostile world without hope? Morrison's books, in particular, with the use of magical realism, brought Africa to my front door and carried me (back) to Africa. She reminded a Black girl like me that Africa resides in me (i.e. the African unconscious); and it is to Africa where we must return to seek out the wisdom (i.e. ancestral knowledge) needed to survive and to enjoy the world we *temporally* (and not only corporeally) inherited.

Soon after reading the story of South African Mark Mathabane, I researched the life stories of African freedom fighters Nelson Mandela, Winnie Mandela, and Bishop Desmond Tutu. Voraciously I read and studied everything about their life stories and struggle. All of their stories together awakened my consciousness to a contemporary Black struggle going on near and afar. No longer was the Black struggle isolated to southern cities in the past, I learned that Black people had an on-going struggle against medical, educational, economic, and political apartheid. Mrs. Fahey does not know that the day she handed me *Kaffir Boy* is the day that she unwittingly radicalized me.

In middle school, I psychologically committed to the politics and philosophy of Black liberation, because through books I was able to associate names and places to a set of policies and practices that served to dehumanize people that looked like me, members of my family, and my neighbors. Many of those policies and practices felt similar to the humiliation and suffering that I witnessed in my neighborhoods in Chicago and the suburbs.

In our Black communities at home, like Black segregated communities in South Africa, schools pushed White teachers, books, and images down our throats; police harassed, beat up, and locked up our Black men; and Black people were homeless and our neighborhoods were overcrowded. Meanwhile, outside of our neighborhoods, White people seem to have plenty; they were the doctors, lawyers, librarians, teachers, police, and they were the ones in charge of our fate as they comprised the local, state, and federal government. My generation was being schooled by White teachers who never mentioned to us that we were Black people, spoke of racial equality, or discussed culture.

On the other hand, reading books on Black suffering and struggles for emancipation demonstrated that not all oppression was overt but often imperceptible. In South Africa and post-chattel slavery U.S.A., at least Black people knew *their place*, so they knew who and what they were fighting against. In contrast, surviving the 1980s and 1990s, my generation did not know *our place* in the world. The school desegregation rhetoric of the 1960s and 1970s, presented as false generosity and handed us false hope. As a result, Black students were *schooled* to be tolerated and to tolerate (White supremacy capitalism patriarchy). Luckily, for me, books named the imperceptible and cultivated an imagination of emancipation.

Know thyself

My high school years were about survival of the fittest (channeling here Mobb Deep!). What my aunt and uncle (my guardians after my mother's death) did not realize when they followed their dreams and bought a house in that collar suburb (small towns that start at the point where the city ends and poor white suburbs begin) of Chicago is that business leaders and the city government had already decided to turn that small town into a ghetto. The plan consisted of encouraging current White homeowners to place their family homes on the market, then a private investor would buy the homes and resell them to Black families at affordable rates. Meanwhile, the city government would turn other older homes in their neighborhood into low-income housing for the poor. As my parents later discovered, the new Black homeowners who purchased their homes would later be burdened with higher interest rates on their mortgages and property taxes.

Black like me

If one recalls in a previous section above, I mentioned that White residents had signs in their windows that read, "Hell no, we won't go". Those signs actually alluded to the fact that White residents were not simply being pushed out by the newly arrived Black residents, but actually by White investors. Private investors and city government conspired to help build racially segregated suburbs far from metropolitan Chicago, while simultaneously profiting off the dreams and aspirations of Black working class homeowners. By the late 1980s, the suburban community where I grew up and attended school was predominately Black with mostly lower-income and working-class families.

A few White families remained and attended the local school until their ticket was called to move on to better opportunities and social conditions. At school, the teachers were not prepared to teach with Black children, and outside of school, city officials were not prepared to serve families plagued with the social problems that accompany generational poverty. Our little suburban neighborhood had become a living and breathing war zone for Black girls like me who knew better and dreamed of better places.

In our little enclave: Boys fought boys, girls fought girls, and boys fought girls; gang members shot at gang members, drug sellers shot at drug sellers, and drug users canvassed the streets for drug sellers; children did not have men in the home, so boys became the man of the house, and 13- and 14-year old girls shared bedrooms with their own babies and little sisters. In the meantime, police officers terrorized boys, girls, drug dealers and buyers, and paid no mind to the children whose psyches became casualties of war. Those Black homeowners who could leave eventually left the neighborhood, and others like my parents who could not afford to leave became role models, other mothers, and leaders in the community. The school environment for some of us became a vehicle up and out of this ghettoized community.

By high school, I had two goals: (1) not to get pregnant, and (2) to graduate high school without becoming pregnant. Girls like me had a love-hate relationship with boys. We wanted the attention of boys, but we also believed that boys brought drama from other girls and put you at-risk of an unplanned pregnancy. Education was a suitable distraction from neighborhood and family chaos as well as risky adolescent romances. So, while my high school teachers wished that I expressed an outward appreciation for Emily Dickinson, Edgar Allen Poe, Shakespeare plays, or Beowulf, I only experienced schooling during those years as an underground railroad of sorts. Certainly, I enjoyed high school, but in reflection, my high school years was a rite of passage full of ups and downs with little to do with academics, but more to do with learning how to adapt to and persist in the face of adversity.

Sister Souljah

By the time I began undergraduate studies, I had already developed a girl-centered Black consciousness, due to family experiences, literature, and hip hop culture. Indubitably, in college, I sought out cultural spaces and books that would further ripened my racial consciousness. Fortunately, the university where I attended undergraduate school had the largest library in the U.S. outside of the Library of

Congress. Interestingly enough, I worked at the library for a couple of years in undergrad. Anyhow, a few books stand out to me as significant in helping me better understand the social world around me and my role in it.

One book that comes to mind is, *No Disrespect* by Sister Souljah. I was already a fan of Sister Souljah's music, when I read her first book. Her ability to connect the Black urban experience to larger structural forces showed me how creative writing and storytelling could be used as a medium to reveal how racism and intra-racial sexism plays out in Black neighborhoods and relationships.

> I was beautiful; after all, my skin was as rich and dark as wet, brown mud, a complexion that any and every pale white girl would pray for – that is, if she believed in God. My butt sat high in the air and my hips obviously gave birth to Creation. Titties like mangoes, firm, sweet, and ready. My thighs and legs were big and powerful, kicking Vanna White and Cindy Crawford to the curb.
>
> (Sister Souljah, 1994, p. 165)

Sister Souljah presents narratives of Black personalities, politics, and relationships as unapologetically messy. Yet, in her musings she avoids pathologizing the Black experience and exhibit it as a human experience. Even more importantly, as exampled in the excerpt above from *No Disrespect*, Sister Souljah affirms in her storytelling the most vulnerable Black woman—young Black women surviving in poor Black urban communities.

Similarly, Malcolm X's autobiography reminded me that Black men were not helpless victims of their circumstances. His life story reminds any change agent to consider agency alongside of oppression. Soon enough any radical learns that is just as important to study the oppressor as it is the oppressed. Dr. Frances Cress Welsing (1991) flipped science itself on its head and exposed the oppressor. More radical brothers and sisters always dropped her name as a must-read. Dr. Cress Wesling, a psychiatrist by trade, blew my mind with the *science* behind racism. In short, I appreciated immensely how she borrowed from biology and physics to explain White people's obsession (or psychological drive) to annihilate Black bodies. She convincingly argued that White is a recessive gene trait while Black is a dominant gene trait; thus, those of European descent have an instinctual drive to kill off melaninated people in order to survive on this planet. Further, Cress-Wesling argued throughout her text using common scientific concepts and euphemisms that White people are psychologically consumed with preventing their extinction. White people's psychological, physical, and biological fragility was evident in everything they ever created from law to architecture to religion, the psychiatrist argued.

Regrettably, this widely read book in Black radical circles is also evidence that science more times than not favor whomever is telling the story. In addition to being formally trained as an academic researcher, I am also a clinical social worker with experience as a psychotherapist. Therefore, I am sensitive to and hyperaware of not only how racism and poverty affects the psyche, but also how science of the mind can be used to manipulate people. Science is subjective, and science can be used as a weapon as well as a narrative.

At present, looking back over the entirety of my undergraduate experience, I can state unequivocally that the formal curriculum alone did not initiate my critical consciousness—it was present in me dormant and coiled like a sleeping serpent. Higher education, however, certainly played a role in my development as a scholar who centers Black feminist thought in research and pedagogy. There are quite a few college learning experiences that have made an imprint on my scholarly identity, but women and gender studies courses definitely shaped my critical thinking. Keeping in mind that for a long time my issues were not about positive affirmation of my racial or cultural identity; my *spiritual intuition* directed me to be more contemplative of gender relationships within and across the Black community. So, debates, dialogue, critical texts, and questions about gender awakened a dormant serpent resting in my core. Political critiques of gender roles and politics of gender in the context of White supremacy patriarchy capitalism was the subliminal call that awakened the dormant serpent.

What have you done for me lately?

In women and gender study courses, I was typically the only Black person present. Everyone else was White and female. Over the course of the semester, we discussed popular culture and conversed on topics like the representation of women in the media, contemplated if pornography demeaned or empowered women, and debated porn's relationship to rape culture.

We were also introduced to the basics of social constructionism in feminist theory, and learned the differences between the terms gender, sex, and sexuality. Besides concepts associated with feminist thought, we also heavily interrogated date rape and relationship violence with special attention to the cycle of violence.

Evidently, a lot of White fraternity boys were raping White college girls. On college campuses the assumed rapist was a White male, and the assumed victim, a White female student. Accordingly, rape culture was addressed from a White perspective. As a result, countless young Black women were left to our own devices to resolve the images and reality of rape culture in our lives.

At the time, besides the very visible sexual exploitation in rap music, my generation was still trying to make sense of: child sexual assault allegations against Michael Jackson (1993), the rape trial of Tupac involving a young Black woman named Ayanna Jackson (1993), singer R. Kelly's alleged romance and marriage to underage teenager singer Aaliyah (1994), and the famous O.J. Simpson trial where the athlete was accused of domestic violence and murder of his White wife (1995). Trust me, for far too many Black girls, child sexual abuse, acquaintance rape, and domestic violence are ignored serious problems within our homes and communities. Yet, no one was addressing violence against our women in culturally responsive ways.

In the meantime, women studies students were introduced to feminist theorists like Virginia Wolf, Elizabeth Cady Stanton, Simone de Beauvoir, Betty Frieden, Gloria Steinem, Andrea Dworkin, and Mary Wollstonecraft. I only later learned that many of the original White women identified as so-called "founders" of the feminist movement were outright racists who asserted White women's rights and bargained off the rights of Black people to gain the vote for themselves.

There was no Black feminist thought class, thus, feminist theorists bell hooks, Patricia Hill Collins, Audre Lorde, Alice Walker, Barbara Smith, and Angela Davis, and other feminists of color, were token reads on the required reading lists. And, of course, we could never read more than one Black feminist in a semester. White students enrolled in the courses, consequently, did not learn much about Black women's epistemology and learned not to take Black women's anti-racist feminist standpoint seriously. Indirectly, I learned that White liberal feminists were not serious about challenging racism in feminist circles or society.

Honestly, I never felt like an outsider in women studies courses as I did in many Sociology (my declared major), and general studies courses. Outside of these courses, attending a predominately White institution (PWI), I always felt insignificant and invisible and vulnerable (due to common racial attacks and violence against women in the larger campus community). Despite comfort and the intellectual stimulation in women's studies courses throughout my academic career, my Black peers found it quite puzzling that a Black girl from the hood would be interested in feminist politics.

Women's studies was viewed as a social space for weird punked out lesbian White girls who did not fit in with the wealthy sorority girls. During the college years, I might have been described by my peers as "the studious, pro-Black, card carrying hip hop/RB, hyper-sensual, hood girl." What would be my interest in anything involving White girls and their issues? Soon enough, which I believe was a sign of growth on my part and the part of my peers, on campus, I simply became viewed as *political* with both a deep passion for gender equality and a vocal soldier against racism.

What my friends did not know, however, is that it was in my first *Introduction to Feminism* course that I began to raise critical questions about racial exclusion in academic discourse. For instance, I raised the question, "Is Janet Jackson a feminist, since Madonna is considered a feminist?" "Black women read and write about gender, why aren't they listed in the syllabus?" And, it was in this first women studies class where I proclaimed, "White women introduced me to the term feminism, but my grandmother showed me how a feminist does." I began to decipher between academic rhetoric and social reality, and theory and praxis.

Stated differently, I learned and accepted (and made it known) that White middle-class women's social reality was ontologically different from that of Black women's reality. The White feminist professors adored me (not in a fetish kind of way either), because I represented the possibility of an amplified gendered body—I was bold and direct in my stance. I did not shrink for anyone's benefit. Of course, at that time, I was too naive to know to shrink.

Another observation that appears minor, but is actually culturally significant, is that women's studies professors always referred to students as "women" in class. For example, the instructor would ask a question similar to this, "Well, what do you women think?" The first time the professor grouped me in as a "woman," I scoped the room to see who she was referring to; I wanted to see if anyone else was surprised that suddenly we became "women." The White students accepted the title "woman" and were empowered by its use. In my mind, not only did the professor see me as something I was not (i.e. a woman), but she inadvertently committed a cultural taboo.

Where I am from, going away to attend college does not make someone a woman. Learning or knowing how to read, write, or do math did not make someone a woman; and certainly, one's age did not make him or her an adult woman. Where I am from, we earned the right to be called *woman* and that was based on the ethos of our culture. I still am shocked when younger college students categorize themselves as *woman* at such young ages, with little experiences or markers of womanhood. Although there is not a book, set of prescribed rituals, or clearly defined definitions of who a woman is in the Black community, there is a cultural distinction made between *girl* and *woman*.

I viewed myself as a girl, and I viewed the White girls around me as *a girl*. Even though I viewed the professor as a woman, I was not convinced that my classmates or me achieved the status of a *woman*. From my cultural frame of reference, being a woman is an earned status, not an acquired status. Womanhood is not something that is simply handed to you at a certain age (e.g. 18 or 21) or a specific moment in life (e.g. going away to college or starting menses). Nor is someone a woman, simply because a White middle-class professor called you a woman. For me, *becoming* a woman was a process. Already coping with the cognitive dissonance generated by the obvious epistemic apartheid (Rabaka, 2010) in women's studies courses and racism in feminist politics, being identified as a woman too soon was surely a precursor to my cultural and intellectual aversion to White feminism.

Frankly speaking, (1) I never gave White women permission to define me, (2) I did not need them to empower me, and (3) it was a disappointment to me that fellow students in the class had already determined that they knew what it meant to be and live like a woman. White women and girls' cultural experiences, values, and ethos shape their perceptions of girlhood and womanhood. It would not have been in my political interests to allow a White woman professor to place onto me an identity (e.g. woman) based on their own cultural frame of reference. To place their conceptualization of womanhood onto my body and psyche would be equivalent to taking on a foreign identity. While they proclaimed to be women, I was still proudly performing a rebellious Black youth identity as political praxis and cultural assertion

Furthermore, one objective of most feminist studies courses is to empower students by intentionally placing women at the center of discussions on gender, sexuality, history, politics, etc. Coming from a racially conscious background and being reared in a community where most women exercised shared power in the home sphere and in community politics, I never felt like I needed someone to *give* me power or authority. Years as an athlete and experiencing multiple stressors as a teen, I felt physically and emotionally powerful, and knew how to use my voice. I needed to learn how to use my voice more conscientiously and strategically to save myself from myself.

Bringing forth

Upon reflection, I yearned for an education that affirmed and enkindled my innate power in order to *become a woman*. Na'im Akbar (1998), in the book, *Know Thyself*, points out that education is derived from the Latin verb educare, which translates to mean *to bring forth* or *to bring up*. Blatantly stated, shit was fucked up back at home! Education was supposed to help me devise a blueprint for helping me help people back at home. Me and those White girls in those women's studies courses were seeking knowledge for different purposes from the jump. I was seeking education (as a series of learning experiences) to ascertain how women (plural to indicate the interruption of the single White woman experience) live, think, and engage in activities (e.g. cultural, social, political, intellectual, and economic participation) to reach their full humanity.

Enrollment in women's studies courses, which I eventually declared an undergraduate minor, served the purpose of studying women so that one day I would know how to perform womanhood morally, ethically, culturally, and politically. To call me a woman too soon in my education journey was in opposition to an ontological understanding of the purpose of education, which was to get to know myself. Black girls and women may view the purpose of education differently from White faculty and students. As a Black girl in those early women's and gender studies courses, I was culturally marginalized because (1) a White middle-class conceptualization of education was prioritized, and (2) my identity as a Black girl could not be affirmed in a setting that was pedagogically and philosophically designed to affirm White women.

Unquestionably, undergraduate curriculum considers the developmental stages of students, which is probably so much emphasis was put on calling those white girls, women. However, one objective of graduate coursework and interactions with faculty is to provide us with mental models and role models. So, imagine cultural marginalization plays out in qualitative research courses where graduate students of color are present.

- How do our research paradigms privilege White middle-class conceptualizations of the purpose of research and science?
- How might our pedagogical choices in the teaching of research methods and science marginalize students of color?
- If from a cultural perspective, education is about "bringing forth one's potential," then how do research faculty take into account students' cultural experiences to bring forth the innate potential of all our students?

I posit here from a Black feminist/womanist standpoint that innate potential is meant to be tapped into to decode and rectify social problems that afflict students' respective communities.

As purveyors of research, students' cultural experiences and intuitive perceptions will shape (1) their choice of research questions, (2) ideas of what is a suitable research problem or issue, (3) approaches to data collection, (4) data analysis, and

(5) choices of research presentation. Akbar asseverates that knowledge is the capacity to know oneself, and to have the ability to communicate that knowledge to others. Are our research approaches reflective of ourselves, and more importantly, are we able to confer such knowledge across contexts where it is most needed?

To conclude, in the study of my own undergraduate experience at a research-intensive institution, and enculturation into feminist studies, one begins to recognize that many Black women researchers, like other researchers of color, heedlessly train to focus on and to solve White people's problems. Black social workers are trained to implement "fix a nigger" projects (a phrase a mother activist shouted out at a research conference to describe the uselessness of academic research in Black and indigenous communities); Black nurses are trained to wipe the asses of old White people (rarely do Black young women ascend to the higher levels of the profession as they are alienated or feel disenchanted); Black doctors are trained to treat Black people based on medical research and trials conducted with White patients; Black business majors are schooled to go out and to make more money for the White elite; Black university support staff are hired to babysit and console White older adolescents in the resident halls as they make dumb adolescent decisions while not being able to accord the same level of protections to students of color on campus. Likewise, Black people hired in college and university diversity programs find themselves simply appealing to the developmental needs of White students as they attempt to implement anything close to multiculturalism.

Similarly, Black scholars find that they are hired to socialize the next generation of young scholars to accept European theories "of the order of things" and to transfer that knowledge of order on to the next generation of scholars. Many of us discover that when we do attempt to deviate from what is expected of us, or deviate from what we were "trained to think" or how we were trained to act, we experience feelings of alienation, and risk loss of tenure and promotion.

In the end, more conscientious scholars, during their tenure, contemplate how to break the chains of intellectual servitude. We must actively strive to decolonize the mind while we simultaneously act to decolonize research methodologies. For me, qualitative inquiry approaches that take place in collaboration with the self and the most vulnerable in society bring us one step closer to intellectual emancipation. The next step in emancipatory praxis in qualitative inquiry is to interpret and represent our various communities' knowledge within and across contexts.

FIELDNOTE 4

TELLIN' STORIES

Black women's thumbprints

It's hard out here for a pimp? Well, try being a prostitute.

~*Venus*

Regina was my best friend in the fifth grade. I thought she was the prettiest, nicest, smartest, and best dressed girl that I had ever met in my entire nine years of life. Her mother made sure that she came to school with her pigtails finely twisted, silky, and shiny. Regina had light brown eyes with light naturally brown-streaked straightened hair that seemed to match her cocoa skin, and what Black folk called back then "hazel eyes." Her breath even smelled like cocoa.

In class, Regina learned easily and quickly. She liked school, even though she came to school crying sometimes. At school, rarely did she discuss the purpose of her tears. Our favorite past time was to complete homework together, and walk to the local library, which was on the White side of town approximately two miles from our home. The White librarians hated our presence for they thought we were too loud and rambunctious.

"If you all keep up the noise, we will ask you to leave." We giggled in unison quietly, and slowly slipped candy out of our book bags and quickly into our mouths.

"There is no food or drinks in the library. You will be asked to leave."

I looked at the librarian sideways and rolled my eyes.

Regina and I, and few other neighborhood friends, could have been the blue-print of today's Barnes and Nobles and other reading cafes. Even though we did not read at the library but mostly socialized, for Regina and I, the library was our cerebral playground. We could not accept that reading was not to be pleasurable or a communal endeavor for us girls.

Unfortunately, the librarians failed to imagine that the library offered more space, light, air conditioning, quietness, and symbols of other worlds than our homes only two miles away in walking distance. We preferred to check out multiple books at once and read at home with less than a week to return the books back to their rightful place—under the watchful eye of the stern White woman who deemed herself as the guardian of the books. Reading stories and other people's scenes of a fictitious childhood and adolescent growing pains was our escape from reality.

When we were not playing school or reading, our other favorite play activity was to dress and comb the hair of brown Barbie dolls. Regina liked to draw images of stylish outfits, and I liked to pretend to be her model. She designed outfits for our dolls, and I was the model of our future fashion design business.

Regina and I sewed her creations together with pieces of garments by hand. The dolls and I would model our fashions with pride. All we needed to create something unique and worthy of praise back then was a sewing needle, a couple spools of black thread, old discarded materials from worn out-grown clothes; and our collective imagination, cooperation, and validation. Imagine intellectual thought as a joyful creation—comprised of the old and out-grown—threaded together and validated within Black girls' communal spaces. Now, imagine Black and Brown girls and women modeling these intellectual creations, publicly and privately. Aha! The artist and her (intellectual) creations are legit!

Dis-obedience

Teachers and my parents thought that Regina was a good role model for me, because she was not only polite, but she was extremely obedient. I am not sure that many people would have described me as obedient. Of course, in the 1980s, all Black girls were required to be polite, with responses like "Yes, ma'am. No, ma'am." However, obedience was not necessarily a quality forced upon us. Black girls were allowed some level of defiance, because disobedience could be a protective factor, against strangers and kin alike.

A girl may have needed to say "fuck you" to a stranger trying to get her attention at the bus stop, or "I'm telling my mama" to an older child or adult attempting to take advantage of her innocence, and "kiss my ass" to the neighborhood antagonizer.

Life as a Black girl at times required *dissing* somebody, as in "dismissing" or actively choosing to be disobedient, depending on the circumstance. My personality oozed of defiance. Cussing, fighting, talking back, clicking my teeth, and rolling my eyes were a part of my personal Black girl repertoire that I carried around stubbornly but proudly.

Regina, on the other hand, was submissive in her interactions with adults, especially her mother. For example, whenever any of our friends would say something hilarious in class, Regina would cover her smile and giggle in her hand. If a teacher caught her laughing, she would immediately apologize, lower her head, smile, and would diligently get back to work.

I liked her as a friend, because she loved learning and was not afraid to show it, and Regina adorned a subtle kind of pretty like me as well. Not stunning, but pretty enough to be some boy's crush, or to receive an unwarranted compliment of adults. Nevertheless, I found Regina to be an oddity, because she did not have that Black girl edge. Meaning, that she was not assertive in her stance or openly defiant when she needed to be, like many other Black girls in my neighborhood. If a teacher, another student, adult, or stranger pushed me enough, I rarely hesitated to respond accordingly.

For example, once in the third grade, an older girl named Shondra moved next door to our family home. Shondra was in the third grade too, but she was two years older than us, and about 20 pounds heavier than me, and at least four inches taller (at least this description fits my eight-year-old imagination). The girl and her family were known to have gang affiliation. For months Shondra bossed (a term used back then in place of today's term bully) me around.

"Venus, steal that candy." I stole the candy for Shondra.

"Venus, give me your candy necklace." I handed over to Shondra my candy necklace.

Whenever Shondra demeaned, pushed, or taunted me, I did not strike back out of fear that I might not be able to handle a physical attack with her. However, the day that I did strike back was the day that she threatened to kick my little sister's ass.

Although my younger sister was, and still is, taller and thicker than me, my sister was extremely shy and quiet. My sister was a selective mute. She only spoke to immediate family members and close friends. Being the protective older sister, when Shondra made that public threat, and organized all the neighborhood kids to witness the beat down, my fear quickly erupted into rage. My own mother thought that I was too much of a fighter, and that my sister needed to learn how to fight her own battles. In the hood, boys and girls are taught that they have the right to stand up for themselves from bullies.

In my mother's words, "She better learn to fight for herself, or she gon' be gettin' her ass kicked the rest of her life."

Like Regina, my sister did not have the fighting spirit in her. Therefore, even though my mother pleaded with me (better yet, threatened me) not to fight on behalf of my sister, at the public gathering in our backyard, I stood in the place of my sister and whooped Shondra's tail.

Before the neighborhood instigator could hold out her hand and speak the words, "Hit my hand first if you bad," I pounced on Shondra like a wild tiger. Immediately after the fight, Shondra congratulated me "for not taken no shit," and she declared to her neighborhood cronies, "Venus, am yo' bodyguard. Ain't nobody gon' mess with you. Respect."

Once again, Black girl defiance and tenacity was rewarded in our too often hostile neighborhood. Yet, in Regina's personality, I could not find Shondra or me. Of course, one is shaped by biology and environment. Shondra was born into a violent family and raised in a dangerous neighborhood. She moved into our neighborhood from the Cabrini Green Housing Projects, which was notorious in the 1980s for violent crimes and gang violence.

When Shondra moved in next door to my childhood home in Englewood, her mother was already doing time in prison, so her father was raising her as a single parent. Shondra had the privilege of attending school when she desired. At least that is what she boasted to friends.

Rumor had it that her mother was locked up for selling drugs. Her father raised her and her two brothers whom were both openly affiliated with the Gangster Disciple (the GDs) gang as teens. Shondra at times claimed to be a GD too. The gang association stood out to me, because most guys in the neighborhood were down with the Black Stone Rangers (or the Stones); thus, we viewed the GDs as naturally grimy and enemies that did not belong in our neighborhood.

Another memory that I have of Shondra's family is of her brothers being arrested after breaking and entering through an attic window in our family home and stealing various items over time. Fortunately, we had a cat named Lady, who one day accidently showed us how she was escaping out of the house. Apparently, the attic window made for a convenient entry and exit point for the cat, thanks to our clever neighbor boys who kept the window open so that they could too enter and exit our house as they pleased when we were away from home. Our cat, Lady, who I had the distinct pleasure of naming, finally solved the mystery of stolen video games, television, a radio, clothes, and other unnoticeable items (only discovered during the police raid).

Anyhow, violence and criminality in her immediate surrounding environment molded Shondra into a juvenile delinquent with her own sense of order and justice. To this day, I empathize with who Shondra was becoming at an early age. Looking back on my own childhood, much of my aggression was in reaction to having to survive a context filled with Shondras, people like her brothers, and family friends and relatives self-medicating and attempting to cope with joblessness, underemployment, educational disenfranchisement, unsafe housing, unplanned pregnancy, depression, and anger.

In fact, a year after the fight between Shondra and me, my own mother died as a result of a house fire. The exact house and attic that Shondra's brothers found to be a gold mine is where my mother's story seems to begin and end for me. All we know is that the fire was started in the attic.

I don't know what made me wake up. I just sat straight up. When I opened my eyes, the room was pitch black, but clouded with thick grey smoke. Immediately, I started to let out slight coughs back-to-back. Something was tickling my throat. Instinct made me hold my breath and not to take deep breaths. I thought back to school lessons: Don't open the door, get on the floor, and try to find an exit. I searched for my brother and sister.

All three of us shared a bedroom and shared a double bed. My eyes could not really see them, but I was able to make out their silhouettes. I crawled over the bed to them. Before long, my ten-year-old brother took his bare fist and bust out the storm window. Glass went flying everywhere—my eyes, mouth, nose, face, hair … My brother forced my sister onto the roof, and I followed her instinctively. Neighbors screamed for us to jump off the roof onto a mattress, because there was no other way to go down from the roof.

Human instinct demanded that we not be that stupid. The mattress was too far away and too small of a target. Smoke rushed out the window onto the roof. My brother's hand was gushing blood. People were screaming and crying out to god and us. Finally, a neighbor from across the street climbed up a railing that led from the porch to the roof and carried us down one by one on his hip.

First my little sister, then me, and last my brother. The fire department finally arrived and we were taken to the hospital. It was at the hospital while doctors poked needles everywhere and picked glass out of my skin that my godmother turned to me and said, "Yo' mama didn't make it, baby."

Liminal spaces

My brother, sister, and I survived the fire, but my mother died of smoke inhalation in the hospital. It was some months after that tragedy that the family moved to the south suburbs of Chicago where I met a softer me, Regina. That softness was not in me, and I knew that early on. Even now, in reflection, I know for sure that I spent the adolescent years one coin flip away from incarceration, school dropout (or school push out), early pregnancy, or being a domestic violence victim.

Being hard when I needed to be was a protective shield. I judged Regina as *soft* compared to myself and other Black girls. We were best friends, because she respected my sassiness and I her softness. Black girls were not allowed to be soft, right?

Even in middle school, I surmised that Regina's softness came from somewhere or someone beyond herself, just as I understood that Shondra's hardness came from outside of herself. In fact, most girls I knew fell somewhere between Regina and Shondra. They were more similar to me—existing in the liminality between softness and strength and vulnerability and resistance.

Regina soon began to exist in this liminal space of Black girlhood. As her best friend and confidant, I learned that Regina's mother shacked up with a couple of drug dealers throughout Regina's childhood. When her mother was drunk or high, the boyfriends would sometimes flirt with Regina or her sisters. By the time we were in middle school, Regina had already been a victim of child molestation at the hands of the male friends of the family.

One time when we were about 11 years old, one of her mother's boyfriends kissed and molested her while she was asleep in her bed. When Regina tried to tell her mother about the incident the night after the molestation occurred, Regina's mother got angry and called her a liar.

"Did you tell someone?" I gently asked, while knowing that Black girls don't tell.

"Nope. My mama will kill me. She tell me don't be tellin' her business."

"What she say when you told her?" The only question I could ask realizing that I too was now sworn to secrecy.

"She ain't gon' believe me."

Regina did eventually disclose to her mother about the sexual advances and flirtatious gestures of one of her mom's man friends. Considering that Regina and her mother were only 14 years apart in age (and her maternal grandmother was 14 years older than her mother), I became used to hearing allegations of jealousy and sabotage. Mother and daughter both accused the other of jealousy.

As we aged, the rage between Regina and her mother became more persistent and violent. To me, it was like once Regina began her period, her mother began to talk to her and treat her like a grown woman. The period that we begged would come and bless us with the womanhood graces of Mother Nature would eventually become a curse for too many of us Black girls. Our female caregivers seemed to look at us differently, as if they knew something about ourselves that we did not know.

Even today, for instance, I am not sure if subtle physical transitions (i.e. boobs, popping booties, and periods) caused Regina's mother to either view her own daughter as competition getting in the way of male attention, or did the demarcation of the transition from girl to fertile girl-child cause her mother to see Regina as a gullible woman-child in need of harsh discipline to protect her from the masculine gaze. Or, maybe I cannot simply accept that there are mothers and other adults who actually blame their daughters for boys' and men's pathology?

In the summer after we turned 12 years old, I went to visit Regina at her house. The doorbell did not work, so I opened the screen door and knocked on the front door made of wood. I could smell food cooking and hear music blaring from loud speakers. Pulling on a cigarette, Regina's mother opened the main door and spoke through the screen door.

"What the fuck do you want, Venus?" She smiled as she slowly sounded out my name. I became accustomed to Regina's mother's shrewd tongue and virulent attitude toward me. Regina confided in me that she did not like me. Her mother referred to me as a *bulldagger* behind my back.

"Hi, Miss Jackson. Can Regina come outside?"

She took another pull on her cigarette and exhaled. The smoke passed through the screen and out into the air over my head, and stated roughly, "Regina on punishment."

Miss Jackson left the interior door open, but turned her back on me and walked away without any other words.

I rolled my eyes, but hoped she didn't see me.

Discipline and control

Three days later, Regina was at my front door. She had a long dry dark reddish scratch on her face that stood out on her brown skin. We sat on the doorstep and talked. She informed me that a few days before that her mother had been drinking. After dinner, her mother told her to clean up the kitchen. Even at the age of 11, Regina was in charge of helping cook and clean for the family. She was also responsible for her younger siblings.

We Black girls referred to this in conversation as "housework we gotta do," but others outside of the Black family might refer to it as child slavery. Many Black girls begin to do housework around the age of seven, and unlike our middle-class counterparts, there were serious consequences to not completing chores correctly. Being a good cook and cleaner prepared the girl for being a good wife. To not complete our chores wholeheartedly or to speak against the unfairness of gender roles got us labeled as disrespectful.

If Regina or any of her siblings were thought to be disrespectful, her mother would quote the bible to remind them of their sins, curse, and hit if warranted. As Regina described sitting on my front doorstep, that night after dinner and drinking, when her mother demanded that she "go clean up the kitchen," Regina responded back to her mother, "I cleaned up the kitchen."

Her mother snapped back, "Who the fuck you talkin' to?" and accused Regina of "talking back." Once again, her mother became predictably violent.

According to Regina, she responded to her mother in a most humbled voice, "Mama, I'm not talkin' back. I'm just telling you that I already cleaned up the kitchen."

Apparently, Regina's mother felt like her daughter was being insolent and "showing off" in front of her mother's boyfriend. As Regina explained it, her mother grabbed her long dangling ponytail swiftly, wrapped it around her hand, and persisted to drag her up a flight of stairs.

As Regina cried and screamed out in pain, her mother commenced to hitting, punching, and calling her a "bitch." When Regina began to defend herself by guarding her face and body, and attempting to push her mother away, her mother then accused her of "acting grown" and trying to fight her back. Once they were upstairs, Regina confided that her mother tried to throw her out the second story window. Supposedly, it was at this point that her mother's boyfriend stated that her mother had gone too far, and he broke up the "fight." After the altercation, Regina was placed on punishment for being disrespectful and "thinking she was grown."

Grown folks' business

Throughout our adolescent years, as we moved neighborhoods, schools, friends, and lost and regained contact, our shared stories of tension, violence, and struggle continued. Regina shared stories that involved alcohol, drugs, flirtatious boyfriends, and verbal and physical confrontations. Regina remained attached to school, remained well groomed, smiled a lot, and earned average or above grades in school. Eventually, in high school, she began to date older boys, skip school, and engage in sex.

Her teenage relationships were adult-like. She spent long hours with her boyfriends, spent overnight and weekend visits with boyfriends, lived with boyfriends, and engaged in unprotected sex. Regina's mother never chastised her for having sex, but she was insistent on Regina not becoming pregnant before leaving from under her roof. She did not want to be a grandmother at her age. By the time the high school years ended, Regina and I were living two different realities of adolescence. Regina was dealing with grown folks' problems in comparison to the teenage relationship drama I whined about daily.

High school phone calls with Regina:

Phone call 1: Hey, Venus. My mama still crazy. I live with my boyfriend. I'm happy.

Phone call 2: What's up, girl. I'm still with this nigga. I think I'm pregnant.

Phone call 3: Chile, this muthafucka been drinkin. I told him he keep gettin' drunk, I'mma break up with him.

Phone call 4: I'm back in my mama house. He be gettin' violent when he drunk. I don't need that shit in my life. I'm tryin' to work and go to school.

The Regina that I knew in middle school had changed by the time we entered our late teens and early 20s. She was easily angered, untrusting of boys, and only appeared happy when she was in a relationship with a boy. Her boyfriends tended to be older than her and misfits. They were men, we were girls. We were still attempting to figure out how to navigate our family relationships, neighborhoods, and schools as Black girls. These older boys/men took advantage of Regina's and other girls search for direction in a social world that devalued Black girls and women. Hell, maybe Regina and other girls took advantage of boys with cars, money, shelter, and prowess.

Somewhere on the road of Black girl adolescence, I lost my strength. I targeted the nice guys—they had to come from a good stable family, show signs of wealth, enjoy schooling, and have access to transportation. I intentionally coupled myself with the cool guys who were simultaneously nerds and athletes (i.e. popular). After being scared by a couple of bad boys, I only wanted to date boys who had as much to lose (or gain) as I did.

History with bad boys:

Bad boy 1: Eighth grade. I was only 13, and he was five years older than me. I enjoyed flirting and kissing him. He walked me to his bedroom. I thought we were making out, aggressively (and passionately, right?) like you see on Beverly Hills 90210. He pulled up my skirt. I said no. He put his dick in anyway. I stared at my ceiling for the next few weeks wondering if I was still a virgin. I learned a couple weeks later that this nigga was actually on probation for rape of a minor. I never told anyone.

Bad boy 2: Freshman year. I am thinking about having sex with Tyrone. Then, Taunya surfaces from out of nowhere and arrives at my school locker after school. "My name is Taunya. Tyrone is my man and my baby daddy." I have been dating Tyrone for four months. When did he have the time to have a baby? Scared straight.

Bad boy 3: Sophomore year. "Hey, we been kickin' it for a while now. You gon' suck my dick?" "Hell no. I don't suck dick." "Come on, girl, it's natural." He immediately took me home, and I did not receive a phone call from him again. In Spanish class, he acted like I was just another face in the classroom. I was dumped for being an unworldly good girl, and not the tough street savvy Black girl that the boys wanted present behind shut bedroom doors and locked car doors, evidently.

Needless to say, Regina and I both experienced growing pains through the adolescent years. However, due to a compilation of a poor mother-daughter relationship, childhood sexual abuse, physically and emotionally abusive teen relationships, it later became difficult for Regina to trust anyone, even herself. Anger and depression became a part of her personality. Today, Regina has a functional and respectful relationship with her mother, and she is a mother of two. She is also a college graduate with multiple post-graduate degrees. Regina's life work consists of helping lower-income mothers identify resources within themselves and their communities to help foster a healthy and high quality of life for the mother and her children. Today, I am a university scholar-activist with the platform and skills to tell our stories.

Fast forward

Today, I imagine a world where Black girls and women are not stuck only reading other people's stories, fictitious childhoods, and perceptions of social life. We deserve a diversity of representations of the theoretical, perceptual, and lived experiences of people who live, worship, and play like us.

Along these same lines, we should not have to perceive White, middle-class, educated women as the guardians of literacy and knowledge. White women have come to represent what is girlhood, female representation of oppression and liberation. Where are Black women's narrations of objectification/subjectification, agency, vulnerability, resilience and resistance? There is a need for more contemporary representations and theorizations of Black girls and women's lived experience through a cultural framework imagined and produced by Black women (and girls) for Black girls and women.

Like our reading and other educational pursuits were in childhood and adolescence, writing and reading the lives of Black girls and women should be pleasurable and communal. Methodologically speaking, writing and reading the lives of Black girls and women must be conversational. Our experiences is a *stew*, dynamic, synchronous, and complex. A stew fermented (or is the word simmered? No, fermented.) in Africanness, southern and urban rebellion, Black girlhood (i.e. Black girl magic) and Black womanhood or the Black feminine divine. Living at the intersections of race, class, and gender, our social, emotional, and cultural experiences require theoretical and methodological interpretations developed in relationship to other women and girls from similar backgrounds and social spaces. In other words, our creations must involve collective imaginations, cooperation, and validation. Validation of interpretations of our shared research, lived experiences, and stories must derive from a collective imagination and cooperation.

Research and writing practices by Black women should be witnessed as subtle acts of disobedience and defiance against race and gender (and age) oppression. The question for scholars (and active readers) is how do we evaluate the authenticity of Black women's stories and truth claims, especially considering the diversity in Black girls' and women's experiences, based on age, geographical location, socioeconomic status, sexuality, birth order, religion, family structure, physical aesthetics, language, physical and intellectual abilities, etc.? Dis/obedience may be a determining factor in how authentic or critical a womanist (Afro-centric and woman-centered) scholar text is to audiences. Is the text transformative? Does the text push back against the status quo? Does the author's stories (or other art) portray a protection for the weaker and meek in her own community or other marginalized communities? Is there a call to action, either subtly or boldly? Who is being called to action, insiders or outsiders of the community or communities discussed in the text?

In the spirit of Black feminist thought, hopefully both insiders and outsiders are asked to change some kind of undesirable practices or policies that might be deemed harmful to the most vulnerable. In social justice work, there is a need for individuals who have a fighting spirit; those who are able to identify, name, and creatively confront racial and gender injustice in ways that affirm Black girls' and women's humanity. Affirmation comes from acknowledging Black women's ways of knowing, cultural expressions, Black vernacular, and cultural speak.

Unfortunately, academic English is limited in capturing certain aspects of Black woman dialect. For example, in the stories above, it is difficult to capture a Black woman's eye roll, smack of the lips, sounds made in the back of the throat, smacking of the lips, or tongue click.

All of these various non-verbal communications have significant meaning to many Black women. Furthermore, these types of non-verbal expressions have different meanings depending on the context, timing, age and status of communicator, duration, etc.

For example, in the above reflection, I mentioned how a girl child rolled her eyes. We might ask the questions: Did the girl roll her eyes in class or on the playground? Did she roll her eyes during conversation or had the conversation already ended? Did the girl roll her eyes at an adult or at her peer? Was the eye roll quick or slow and exaggerated? Because different behaviors have various meanings, depending on the cultural context, it would take cultural insiders to determine the authenticity of an occurrence. Cultural insiders with a unique gendered cultural orientation and frame of reference like Shondra, Regina, or Venus. Also, it would take scholars who are committed and bold enough to attempt to convey Black women's experiences in culturally affirming ways, despite the linear and static conventions of academic English writing.

Black women's shared stories and interpretations of our lived experiences convey a sense of sympathy and empathy of Black girls' and women's multiple realities. In the storytelling process, there is a sense of feeling respect and compassion for another woman's experiences. Moreover, is it obvious that the author thought about what it was like to walk in a character's shoes, or has the author engaged in storytelling that results in the audience imagining what it is like to walk in the various characters' shoes as raced, classed, and gendered bodies?

Methodologically, we want to produce emotionally stimulating texts alongside culturally affirming texts that serve to affirm our humanity. These cultural productions strive to capture vulnerability and resistance. In actuality, most Black girls' and women's existence fall in the liminal space between vulnerability and resistance. The liminal space of our existence is a state of resilience. Most of us simply *maintain* and try to survive, sort of speak, until we are encouraged, introduced to and learn to continually and purposefully engage in acts of resistance. Researching, theorizing, and writing, are acts of resistance. Deciding to live is an act of resilience and resistance.

To share our stories, in oral or written form, requires mutual trust between (1) the person sharing the story, (2) the listener of the story, (3) and the audience receiving the story. In Regina's story above, or my interpretation of the story, Regina began to trust me in understanding her story at an early age. Her survival was based on having someone to share with, and she intuitively trusted me to be a good listener and confidant. Nearly 30 years later, she now trusts me to tell her story based on how I remembered it being told to me, but also she trusts me to use my academic knowledge and storytelling skills to share her/our story outside of friendship.

Today, Regina and I both have decided to trust that readers will not judge her/our story, generalize (or stereotype) our story as every Black girls' reality; and that readers will be moved to action to assist Black daughters in creating safe spaces to develop to their full humanity; or at the least become aware of how they themselves might be willingly or unwillingly creating barriers to our *coming forth*. We trust the audience of our stories will be able to draw upon their own knowledge, skills, talents, and resources to help Black women scholars acquire resources and supports needed to serve as our community's griots, truth tellers, and revolutionaries. Our intellectual and cultural pursuits allow us to move beyond being the *keepers of secrets* to being scholar-activists who choose to use our secrets to instigate social and community transformation. In other words, daughtering prepared us, willfully or unwillfully, for intellectual activism and cultural preservation.

FIELDNOTE 5

(DE)COMMODIFICATION OF THE BLACK GIRL NARRATIVE

Prologue

Why I need Black feminism?

I need Black feminism ... because I was born into a house where Black women were honored for their beauty, style of dress, how they adorned their hair, dance moves and how smoothly they could switch their ass from side to side.

I need Black feminism ... because I grew up in a house where women were praised for talking shit, smacking lips, and snatching wigs. I also grew up in a house where women were expected to cook, clean, grocery shop, take care of the kids, take care other people's kids, iron, wash the laundry, and play spades, bid wiz, and gin rummy.

I need Black feminism ... because I also grew up in a house where daddy got the first plate, even though he didn't make his own plate, and he got the last piece of meat, and he was the only one allowed to put his feet on the couch.

I need Black feminism ... because in my neighborhood a girl or a woman child can be called a bitch or a hoe, but to call a boy or a man a bitch, hoe, pussy, punk, or fag is fighting words. Plus, the same dudes who didn't like to be associated with female body parts could choose at any moment when to pop his baby mama, girl-friend, or wife in the mouth for "not watchin' your mouth" or "forgettin' who the fuck you talkin' to" or "actin' like a bitch."

I need Black feminism ... because when I was seven I saw my uncle, as we say in Black vernacular, jump on my auntie, before that we only heard screams and crashes from behind closed doors.

I need Black feminism ... because when I was eight, during a neighbor friend's sleepover, in the middle of the night, her drunk father came home and beat his wife in front of us, threatened to shoot her and himself with a gun.

I need Black feminism ... because when I was eight my godmother's teenage brother directed me into the bathroom and told me to suck his dick! I need Black feminism, because I was grown before I even told anyone.

I need Black feminism ... because when I was nine my best friend, walking home from school, told me that her father "stuck his thang" in her "stuff" the night before.

I need Black feminism ... because I was only nine and a half when my mother, tired of the drunken fights and sexual innuendos, took me and my siblings in the middle of the night, with pajamas on, to her friend's house; ran away from my dad on a Greyhound bus back to her home town.

I need Black feminism ... because at the age of ten, my best friend's mother, who insisted I was a dyke, dragged her, beat the shit out of her, and tried to throw her out a second story window, after my friend informed her beloved mother that her cocaine induced boyfriend had tried to rape her the night before; the same boyfriend who openly flirted with us on the daily.

I do not just need Black feminism to help me deal with all this shit. I need Black feminism ... because I yearn for a socio-political praxis that teaches me how to fight the oppression of Black girls and women as raced, classed, and gendered objects in a world that values men over women, White over Black, and wealth over poverty.

I need Black feminism to breathe air from my lungs to the lungs of another sister to help her live ... more free.

~VEW, 2017, Pedagogical Reflection, Why I Need Black Feminism

More than ten years ago, I began to discuss the education and schooling of Black girls. Besides Black feminist scholar Joyce Ladner, there were not many Black women scholars discussing the socio-emotional and educational development of Black girls from a strength-based perspective (a term derived from the social work literature). Most research on Black girls in education and sociology used quantitative methods to study Black girls, and from a deficit and pathological perspective. Researchers studied everything from Black girls' school dropout rates, teen pregnancy, obesity, gang involvement to smoking cessation.

As a graduate student, I knew even then that most Black girls were not thinking about or worried about those issues. Those were White people's problems; or at the least, White people's problems with us. Most of the Black girls I knew were more worried about how to survive family drama and how to get through school without beating somebody's ass and getting suspended, becoming pregnant by some boy, earning enough credits to graduate on time, and getting a good grade point average to go to college. Most of us did graduate high school, and we graduated with our class. As a grad student, these are the stories that I wanted to tell. I wanted to discover and share how Black girls were navigating their families, school, and communities, in the face of patriarchy, poverty, and racial, class, and gender bias in schools. I accomplished this from an intersectional lens.

Although my academic mentors applauded my ingenuity, I soon learned that this area of scholarly interest could be career suicide; for I was studying Black students, Black girls, poor Black girls, and using qualitative inquiry. Yet, for me, we were worth the risk and our stories were beautiful, creative, resilient, that deserved to be told. I was, nonetheless also, airing our dirty laundry.

Once I was asked one of my committee members while writing my dissertation, "How much of my own story do I tell?"

She responded, "As much of it that you feel comfortable sharing." Since completing my dissertation my original ethnographic research with Black girls has resulted in two editions of the book *Teaching Black Girls: Resiliency in Urban Classrooms*, released in 2005, and again in 2011.

Fast forward.

Approximately three years ago, I was invited to serve as a Roundtable Chair at the American Educational Research Association meeting. The topic was on communities of color and literacy, or something to that extent. Present were mostly graduate students from culturally and linguistically diverse backgrounds; however, there was one White woman presenter who announced that she expected to receive her doctorate in two weeks. She shared her research on an after-school book club for high school Black girls. I cannot remember the details of the presentation, because I went numb after her introductory words:

"Looking at a booksellers list, I found that Black girls read, but they read junk! So, I went to the bookstore and chose books for them."

Scratch the record.

My mind went blank. As the Chair of this conference session, my job was to introduce everyone and keep track of time. After one sentence, I made up my mind that this chick's time was up. I went blank. Other conference participants commended the graduate student on her intervention work. I cringed. The White female savior was being applauded while those poor Black trash reading illiterate Black girls were being bastardized. Once the session ended, the woman told me how she loved my work and it inspired her and said, "Thank you."

But, her acknowledgement opened up space for criticism:

> Did you know Black women are one of the largest consumers of books in this country? Instead of purchasing books at a bookstore that most of those girls don't have readily access to, maybe you can take them to a school or local library to pick out a book. Have you thought about asking them what books they read, why they choose to read particular genres of books, and what stories or characters they relate to and not relate to in those books?

After my subtle, but intentional, interrogation, the woman was visibly scarred by my lack of praise. To this day, I ask myself, "Why was I so irritated with her research?" The graduate student's presentation raised questions about:

1.   Who can research whom? Who legitimates research questions and claims?
2.   Are we imposters on Black girls' bodies and experiences?
3.   In the same way, we ask who gets to define literacy (in all of its multi-facetedness) and good versus bad literary choices, we should also be raising the question of who gets to determine "good" research, ethical research, data, and representation of data as it relates to Black girls and women. Should Black girl *literacies* be considered in data analysis and re/presentations?

4. Is there an anything goes mentality in theorizing and researching young people's, poor people's, and women's lives, as long as good intentions are involved?

The past few years have definitely been the era of the Black girl and Black woman. Thanks to the movement for Black lives, including the Black Lives Matter social movement, Black Youth Project 100 (BYP 100), the Dream Defenders, the Say Her Name Campaign (and the African American Policy Forum), and the organizers (i.e. Black queer women, male and female youth, etc.) behind various youth movements more attention than ever is being paid to the state of Black girls in the U.S.

When I was invited to the White House for a special convening on "The State of Research on Girls & Women" in 2015, there was a racially diverse group of women, but mostly White women, amongst approximately 100 conveners. The phrasing "research on" is usually indicative of well-funded quantitative studies that use instruments created by adults to collect data on girls to later develop or evaluate programs "designed" for girls. To my knowledge, all the Black women present were researching for and with Black girls and young women.

Research with girls entailed locating a social problem or issue relevant to girls and asking them what we needed to do or what program was needed to address the problem. Human potential, human agency, and human experience were at the center of any programming, and research was collective. Our programs were not well funded. In fact, our qualitative research projects and associated programs were rarely funded. Interestingly enough, I later found out that the other Black women present had been introduced to my body of work in their own doctoral programs or Black girls' study work. The White House convening was approximately three years ago.

Since then, with all the new-found attention to Black girls, there has been convening, workshops, and conferences; magazine spreads and news appearances; book deals and journal calls; and social media campaigns around the country in recent years to bring attention to the systematic oppressions that Black girls endure.

Folk are saying, screaming, tweeting, and singing, "#BlackGirlsRock, #Black-GirlMagic, and #BlackGirlsMatter." The question is whose or what scholarship, if any, is feeding these movements and conversations? In this historical moment, is so-called academically "rigorous" research even necessary? What type of scholarship is viewed as worthy of moving forward the movement? What is the role of academicians in a movement that questions all regimes of truth, authority, neutralism, traditionalism, and neoliberal projects? Finally, who is *policing* the Black girl bandwagon as Black girls are being policed?

At such a critical time when Black girls and young women are being policed and pushed out of school, being assaulted and killed at the hands of White vigilantes and police officers, threatened by mass incarceration, neighborhood and media violence, what would be the role of the Black girl researcher? Today, all Black women scholars claim to be a Black girl expert; every Black woman blogger is claiming to be knowledgeable on the Black girl experience; even Black women artists are depicted as knowers of Black girls' lives; hell, even Black men are carving out a niche that claims to know Black girls and women's needs and desires (i.e. Steve Harvey, TD Jakes, and Hill Harper). With so many "knowers" of Black girls' experiences, identities, desires, and pains in the public sphere, what is the moral and ethical obligation of the academic researcher? In the midst of the consumption and commodification of the Black girls' body and experience, these are questions to be pondered.

The flashback

As a college student in late adolescent, there was a yearning in me to not only learn about different ways of life, but also learn about myself. Disappointingly, there was very little on a predominately White college campus, located in the middle of cornfields and more than two hours away from a major Black urban life, that could cultivate a Black consciousness. I was schooled at home that I was Black. I felt gender and witnessed sexual expression openly, but no one talked directly, to young people anyway, about the politics of gender.

Intuitively, I sought out opportunities to express my sentiments and observations about the politics of gender. Fortunately, there were women studies courses embedded across the university curriculum facilitated by women, albeit White women and from a White feminist paradigm. But what is available on college campuses when one sees her skin in the mirror but not on television? When one feels her skin as onlookers stare or look away when she walks into the lecture hall? What was available to help the Black student contend with the surveillance that took place in university towns as she notices that when she walks down Main Street or Campus Street she is invisible, but nearby police officers, restaurant owners, and bartenders see her Black skin not as a college student but as a Black nuisance?

Who or what is there to help her understand scientific racism, when she sits through psychology or sociology classes and her skin is being openly discussed in classes? Or, when one wants to embrace the skin that she is in, and all the cultural baggage, good and bad, that comes with that skin but is subliminally told by the best psychologists, political scientists, economists, historians, anthropologists, and communication professors in the world that her culture is less than and backwards? If education is for becoming, then in those early college years, I yearned for education opportunities that facilitated a Black political consciousness.

In addition to a Black cultural center on campus and a Black student union, there was an African American studies program. The Black cultural center, or what we referred to informally as the Black House, was a site of rich history. From the first time a Black student stepped on campus, she learns about the history of the founding of the Black House. Come to find out, like most traditionally White institutions, the Mid-Western university had a legacy of racial segregation.

Long after Black students were admitted into the university, the university denied housing to its Black students. Oral history tells that Black college students prior to the 1960s were required to seek residency with local Black citizens outside of the university campus; in the midst of the Black civil rights movement, they organized and demanded that the university desegregate campus housing and provide safe cultural spaces for its Black students.

Soon enough the Black cultural center represented a legacy of simultaneously systematic marginalization on campus, Black academic achievement, Black pride, and a material outcome of organized struggle. For some of us, the history of the Black House inception was a tangible reminder that institutions of higher education can be both oppressive and tools of White supremacy. Yet, the cultural center was also a constant reminder that students have a right to demand more from those whom purported to provide us with an education.

The Black House was adorned with Black and African-centered art, newspaper clippings of important historical events and achievements of its founders. It was also a place where university staff and students held meet and greets for new students, Black cultural events like poetry readings and music, and Black student organization meetings. Some of the organization meetings planned ways to organize against institutional practices. Of course, students also gathered to simply chill, talk shit, and shoot the breeze.

I believe that I visited the Black House only a few times in my entire college experience. Blackness for me was multidimensional and complex and extended beyond attire, poetry, and music. Those who frequented the Black House needed or wanted community to affirm their Black identity and to support their ways of cultural expression. However, I arrived on campus with a group of students from my high school. Our little clique represented the high achievers, athletically inclined, and socially astute students (or what was referred to as cool nerds) of our high school. Actually, based on my experience, I argue that it is best practice for college and university admission offices to admit racial/ethnic minority students into the college with other individuals from their high school or neighborhoods. I am sure that beginning college with friends and other students from my previous high school made the transition from high school to college smoother for me. It also meant that it was not necessary for us to hang out and vibe at the Black House to protect our psyche or share our political views.

I had a natural support group who knew who I truly was and could support my true identity in that very White space. And, when someone knows your authentic identity, they will hold that person accountable to themselves and the community. For example, it is not unusual to hear a Black person say to a friend, "Girl, you acting like them White fools?" or "Girl, you got that from them White folks?" The purpose of college is to socialize young citizens into the larger society's culture, economic, and political system.

Black students needed the Black House to preserve their identity in the same way that I needed my friends to preserve my true identity. What many Black students knew, even if we were not able to articulate it at the time, is that the unstated purpose of education was to attempt to socialize students into White culture, capitalism, and to proliferate a political system that benefited the White majority group. Not much on our college campus introduced us to larger Black culture or celebrated it.

There were no Black church services present on campus, no photos of famous Black alumnae, no southern or traditional Black meals (e.g. fried chicken, greens, deep dish cheese macaroni, peach cobbler, etc.) served in cafeterias; there also were no African-centered art, statues, or Black figures displayed around the campus grounds; no R&B, hip hop, or jazz playing in the student union, and only a handful of Black professors on a campus with more than 30 thousand undergraduates.

Alternatively, there were White churches on campus or near campus of nearly every denomination with White leaders and a predominately White congregation. At nearly every turn on campus there was a statute, artwork, Latin script, or photo celebrating European culture, a White historical figure, or alumnus. Also, there were plenty of entertainment and leisure activities to cater to White students, for there were as many campus bars as there were churches. I used to wonder if White students simply left the bar, walked next door to church to pray, and then walked over to the bookstore to read.

Local bars played music that appealed to their White patrons' sensibilities. Blaring from their doors one could hear punk, hard rock, and contemporary White artists. It was common knowledge that bar owners would intentionally avoid playing Black artists or hip hop and R&B music, because they did not want to attract a Black crowd. Besides being selective of what music to play, bar owners used other tactics to keep Black students out, such as the implementation of dress codes (i.e. no jeans and sneakers), front door cover charges, or requiring university issued student identification cards and a driver's license. These policies could easily filter out some Black students at a historical moment when we were exuding hip hop youth culture, paid our own way through school and living expenses; thus, could not afford a vehicle, so we did not need a license.

On campus, there were dozens of White fraternity and sorority sponsored houses that looked like mansions sitting on top of plantations, but there were no Black fraternity or sorority houses on campus. Even the university's recreational programs catered to the tastes of White and elite culture with activities available, like golf, polo, tennis, equestrian club, squash, and archery. Many times when Black students did play the music we liked or gathered in small groups in our dorm rooms, White students reported us to the resident hall director or called the police.

At any rate, Black students knew for sure that White culture was being promoted, we were being socialized into White culture, and the goal was to have us leave mimicking White culture. If we, in any way, displayed signs of rejecting White culture (e.g. speech, aesthetics, or tastes), then we were marginalized or even reported to and punished by the overseers of White culture. In college, race became deeper than skin complexion; it became a performance and a politic. One was either acting (performing) Black or acting White. One was either actively resisting (politicking) Whiteness or passively accepting Whiteness. White students also took on a reactionary stance.

For example, if a course centered the Black experience, White students avoided the class like a plague. If the Black student union sponsored an event, White students would not even bother to show up to participate in the event. And of course, if a

Black student ran for a student government position, most White students would not give attention to the platform the student was running on in the election, because the student was not White.

Consequently, a Black student was rarely able to even make it onto a student government ballot. It was like saying that student government, like homecoming court, was for Whites only. In hindsight, many students were stuck in a cultural and intellectual lag, because they were immersed in a cultural climate on campus that required them to construct their identity in relation to White culture; a campus culture that required us to accept or resist Whiteness and elite culture.

Personally, I did not find it necessary to avoid White people or White culture, which was inescapable because white was all around us. Quite frankly, we were swimming in the proverbial fishbowl of whiteness. Constantly attempting to avoid White people or resist White culture would be cutting off your nose to spite your face. White people do not own education nor knowledge; we are only led to believe that they possess and are the guardians of both.

Racial polarization threatened to stymie my own and other students' critical consciousness and positive racial development. To survive culturally, spiritually, and intellectually, I simply embraced an oppositional identity that opposed any forms of oppression and injustices. I did not have a disdain for White people, but I had a disdain for cultural hegemony. I pursued an education that taught me how to struggle against various forms of oppression to become a better person and active citizen.

Admittedly, as an undergraduate student, I swallowed up White culture—not a White identity—that window dressing was not appealing to me. Rather boldly, I asked White students directly about their musical tastes, family life, and about their religious practices; I inquired about their thoughts on non-Whites, and I even leisurely hung out with a few White students. Interestingly enough, not one friendship that I formed with White students in college lasted beyond college. It seems that for all of us, the friendships themselves were a learning experience at best.

Most of the White students I befriended themselves were cultural outsiders on a campus. One White girl, my second year assigned roommate, grew up in a poor rural community and identified with the punk rock community. She told me that she felt like "a freak" on the elitist campus filled with rich White kids. Another White friend I met was a zealous Christian who attended a multicultural non-denominational church and his father was a mail carrier. He too felt marginalized by other Whites, because he chose not to segregate from racial/ethnic minority students and he could not afford the middle-class style clothes, and he did not perform a middle-class identity. He exuded working class. Another White boy I met, and my friends and I became quite social with, was from a wealthy White family and suburb. I believe his features were just brown enough to feel comfortable blending in with a small group of Black students in our residence hall. His skin tone was kind of a light brown, and his hair thick and dark.

One day while Ahmad and I were chilling in the student lounge, another White guy walked passed us. After the boy walked by, my friend said to me, "Look at that fucking Jew." I was shocked, because I did not know what a Jewish person looked like, and I was shocked at his vehement response to a complete stranger's presence. I followed his comment with, "How do you know he is Jewish?" He responded, "Look at his nose." Without hesitation I responded, "You both look White to me. A nose does not determine someone's racial or religious identity. You are a racist, and if I wasn't sitting here with you, you would call me or another Black person a nigger!"

In response to my quick visibly visceral retort, my friend went on to explain to me that his dad was actually an Arab immigrant. When his father became a citizen, he dropped the last letter of his surname to make it sound more American. After finishing medical school, his father married his mother and they moved to an all-White suburb, and the family settled into their White wealthy suburb and passed as White. Back then, I had no clue about the political and cultural tension between Jewish and Muslim groups. In our brief friendship, I learned about anti-Semitism, White racial socialization, xenophobia, and intra-group White racism.

After his racist rant, I never spoke to him again. I believe that I did not like being taken by surprised that someone could harbor so much hidden hatred toward another human being, especially based on someone's physical features or religion. He had also introduced me to another form of bigotry, which made the world become more complex for me. Many of these everyday "normal" interactions with others whose experiences and cultural beliefs were different from my own showed me over and over again that the social world, or power and oppression specifically, is complex and pervasive.

In my mind, a college education was not about spending my college years fighting White people. White people do not own knowledge or education, and it is not healthy for Black students to spend every waking moment in the college years combatting the White elite's attempt to try to convince non-Whites that they were insignificant or unworthy of higher education. My quest in college was to claim the type of knowledge that I did not have access to in my family's small low-income suburban neighborhood. I engaged in as many learning opportunities as possible, including bar-b-ques and "Take Back the Night", weed sessions and "Hash Wednesday", Black frat parties and White frat house parties. I listened to and learned from White liberal professors as much as I learned from Black, Latino, and Jewish professors.

Moreover, as I did in schools back at home, I questioned, critiqued, and verbally challenged ideas and theories that I determined did not align with or meaningfully expand my worldview. I can state unequivocally that my mind expanded to accept the diversity of humanity. When recognizing the diversity of humanity, one is able to better appreciate the multiple struggles that exist across individuals, communities, ethnicities, religions, and geographical locations. In other words, my mind expanded and my knowledge of the social world grew extensively. In addition to enjoying the pleasures of a student-centered life, I turned to sociology and political science courses on race, class, and gender. The only African American history class I enrolled in during my undergraduate studies was a class that concentrated on the history of U.S. slavery.

To the surprise of the mostly Black students enrolled in the class, on the first day of class we observed that the instructor was a young White hippyish graduate student. Many of the so-called pro-Black students (i.e. the Black House students) called out the irony on the first day of class. The instructor made a case for why he felt qualified to teach the course, and I secretly commended him on his confidence. In actuality, I found it humorous that a White man was teaching a course on U.S. slavery on a predominately White campus that was racially contentious and segregated.

In my immaturity, I surmised that the man was cocky to place himself in front of a group of students who were sizzling with pride and rage. Not to mention, that more than likely enrolled in the class were students who already possessed knowledge of U.S. slave history, and they only wanted to have their knowledge supplemented or validated. I wondered if the White instructor was going to be able to hold on to his White pride and validate these students' identities as historical beings living under present-day enslavement (i.e. economic, political, and cultural subjugation)?

Full disclosure: I took the stance that he deserved to be the target of those Black students' rage, if he was so prideful and did not know intimately his audience. That is the limitation of academia. There are many intellectuals who know subject matter, but they are not intimately connected to the subject or their perspective audiences. So, I was tickled to death at the thought of the White instructor who was confident enough to believe that his knowledge of the subject (of chattel slavery) would be enough to help him survive the semester.

Despite students' contestation, the instructor stood weekly before an audience that was passionate about learning of their experiences of their ancestors in this country, and they were just as passionate about forming alliances amongst their peers on a sensitive topic like institutional slavery. I found humor in the instructor's naiveté and false confidence, even though I was not as vocal as my fellow students in questioning his presence or motives as the instructor of an African American studies course on the history class of U.S. slavery. I was somewhat disconnected from the material taught, because the physical representation (a White male) was in direct conflict with the mental representation I needed from a developmental perspective; an intellectual who represented emancipation from European colonization, progression from chattel slavery, and freedom from the control of Black bodies and thought.

Another barrier that prevented me from finding myself in that class is reflective in the only time that I openly spoke up in class. Once during a class period the instructor compared slavery in the U.S. to slave systems in South America. After contemplating the readings, I raised my hand, and I stood up before the class and professed my disgust with the instructor's (and White historians') proclamation that one nation's slavery was less inhumane or egregious than another nation's treatment of enslaved people. As an example of his ignorance the instructor once stated, "In the U.S., at least slaves were given provisions such as food and clothing." That comparison was fighting words for me.

His statement revealed that he was morally bankrupt or at the least his approaches to historical analysis was void of moral critique. I shouted out, "Slavery denies another human being's humanity. Are you suggesting that the enslavement of African people is okay in any context?" Before I could even thoroughly make my point, more radical voices in the classes began to critique both the content and the instruction methodology, and our instructor's presence in the class. In that moment, I did not connect with the content or the historian's methodology for teaching African/African American history, but I connected with the students' fervor of collective voice in speaking out against authority.

To see other Black students chime in and support my ideas was rewarding, but even more importantly, to witness Black students to collectively articulate their pedagogical expectations and construct their own learning experience was empowering. At that time, the university did not offer many Black history courses, and what they did offer, I was not truly interested in learning. Some people might find this strange coming from a person who proclaimed to be grounded in her Blackness and in search of becoming more conscious of her inner-being; however, no one would expect a White student to enroll in every European history class offered. Maybe such an expectation does not exist for White students, because Europe or European history and culture is all around them.

When the White child enters school, she learns of the great migration to North America and other parts of the world. Upon entering college, every major theorist cited is European. White students see their culture in the professor and find reflections of themselves in Sir Isaac Newton, Charles Darwin, John Locke, Aristotle, Leonardo Da Vinci, Albert Einstein, and Sigmund Freud. White university students did not need any special classes on their people's history, because their culture and history is the purpose of the institution itself—to preserve and transfer Western and European history. Therefore, people of African ancestry have a choice to make when attending historically White institutions. We are forced to choose to separate into our respective cultural enclaves or to totally engage in the consumption of White culture.

I chose to conscientiously, but cautiously, observe White culture. In the transition to college, I never forgot all the lessons my family instilled in me. Remembering my grandparents' musings on the civil rights movement and their own engagement in local politics, I decided to enroll in political science courses. The study of how the U.S. government worked was less than stimulating, but to this day I am glad that I had the foresight to take a class on the function and role of government in a democracy. I believe political science courses provided foundational knowledge that every active citizen needed to know to participate in national and local politics, but it was not necessary to self-identity. In my opinion, the course I enrolled in, "Introduction to U.S. government," was mere indoctrination into believing that the U.S. has the fairest form of government.

Professors never told us that the elite class had the power to buy politicians, lobby congress, and media to spread propaganda. And that poor people were allowed to vote, but had little voice in shaping legislation or bringing needed change at the macro-level. Political science courses taught university students to be "good" citizens, and there was no better government in the world outside the U.S. If a democratic government failed you, it is because you failed at being a good citizen. Fortuitously, there were political science courses cross-listed with African American Studies and sociology courses. Armed with family stories of Black resistance, as an undergraduate student, I decided to enroll in a class on the civil rights movement.

Most of our class discussions covered past patterns of mass organization movements. I learned much about how our ancestors and elders sacrificed (life, paid labor, and pride) to gain basic human and civil rights. But, I sat in many lectures frustrated, if not disgruntled, because the professor rarely connected past struggles for human and civil rights to what my brothers and sisters were experiencing in the hood back at home and on campus.

On campus, we were still being called niggers, came into contact with few Black professors, and were still not represented in student government. At home, my people did not have access to affordable housing, our schools were racially segregated and overcrowded, police harassment and brutality had cannibalized our neighborhoods. I do believe that the history and lessons acquired in Black political sciences courses were useful to my knowledge growth but at the time, no one insistently and critically challenged us to connect past history to contemporary civil rights struggles.

Maybe many of us could have taken that information on past struggles of structural racism and compared them to present-day forms of racism. Perhaps our professors did not want to upset White students or department chairs, which would upset their chances of tenure, or maybe they hoped we would make the theoretical leap on our own and begin connecting the past to our present condition.

Nonetheless, at some point, I noticed that most of the icons at the center of civil rights narratives were men. So, I asked my African American female professor, "Where are all the women in the civil rights movement? Were they in the church kitchen preparing Dr. King's meals, or were they at the print shop preparing flyers for the march, or were they simply satisfied with marching behind the men folk in heels and dresses?"

I think the professor was excited that I inquired. It was at that point of questioning who was absent that my professor provided me the opportunity to study for a final project, and later independent study, the biographies of women involved in the civil rights movement, such as Coretta Scott King, Rosa Parks, Pauli Murray, Dorothy Height, Septima P. Clark, and Ella Baker.

Instantly and with *a sense of gratification* these women's family stories, education narratives, and ways of organizing and speaking truth to power shaped my worldview. Their spoken and embodied politic to put an end to racism, sexism, and poverty became my war cry. And, their goal to use community education as their weaponry became my agenda for exposing and fighting against contemporary forms of oppression. Finally, I discovered what I was in search of: theoretical and practical approaches to combat racism, sexism, and poverty from a cultural and spiritual standpoint.

Exhibit C: Black Girl Power. Dr. Venus Evans-Winters for Teacher College, Columbia University

Black girl power: education for resilience and resistance

Introductions

First of all, I want to thank each and every one of you for welcoming me here today. And, much respect to Teachers College Columbia for having such a vision to host a conference on the education of Black girls and women. And, many more thanks to the entire TC team for they have been more than accommodating, especially my gracious host, Dr. Monique Lane. She has been more than patient with my late responses to phone calls and emails. Thank you Dr. Lane. One more thing, I have to say, being in a room full of young people and women dedicated to learning, understanding and supporting Black Girls Lives and Education—Matters! As they say in the South African indigenous tradition. I AM Full! I AM FULL,

Home training

More than 20 years ago, when I became interested in researching and writing the lives of Black girls and women, there was very little institutionalized knowledge available on the lived experiences of girls of African ancestry. Most of what I already knew about Black girls was handed down from observing the daily lives of Black women, novels, music; and playing games like double-dutch, spades, dominoes, "tell it like it is" and "find a boy, kiss a boy." (Yes, the apparent neighborhood political opposite of "find a girl, kiss a girl.") Family history and girl games embedded messages into my psyche of Black female agency and the necessity of girls to hold their own.

Attending university studies in the Mid-West, during the 1990s, most of the research on Black girls were altogether null, void, or at best, focused on pathology and deficiency. For example, Research in the social sciences typically focused on teen pregnancy, welfare dependency, obesity, and school dropout. Even when feminist and race scholars attempted to center the experiences of Black girls many fell short, because they could only view Black girls as Black bodies or view Black girls through a gendered body.

Scientific racism and hyper-(in)visbility

Most university scholars were unable or unwilling to view Black girls as simultaneously BLACK and GIRL; and, as a Black girl, aesthetically and symbolically speaking. Consequently, many educational researchers and other social scientists overlooked how Black girls could be both vulnerable and resilient in a society that privileges male over female, White over non-White, and wealth over poverty. Theorists missed the opportunity to explore the role of oppression and individual agency in the socialization and life experiences of Black girls and young women. Black girls' nullification in my psychology and sociology courses, back then, put me on a quest to not only share our stories, but to politicize our stories.

At that time, hypotheses, theories, and assumptions about our lives were derived from Eurocentric Western and patriarchal ideas of what it meant to be Black, poor, and a woman. Most of the conclusions reached about Black girls were developed off the back of eugenism in education and welfare reform (under the administrations Reagan, Bush, and Clinton) policies. Similar to today's scientific climate, the political discourse, postured as science, around Black girls' lives were overly simplistic and narrowed to fit the White middle class popular imagination with the intent either to (a) justify our bastardization and dehumanization or (b) pacify youth's yearning for self-determination and the right to develop into their full humanity. In my undergraduate and graduate studies, scientific inventions were working diligently against Black girls.

In the 90s, being inspired by hip hop's celebratory Black female sexuality, calls to fight the power, house party hip hop and gangsta rap music, I knew for sure that Black girls' possessed multiple identities that would require complex social and scientific thought. Yet, I was mostly coming into contact with studies and classroom rhetoric where researchers relied on simplistic and linear notions of race, class, gender and sexuality. However, my grandmother, Janet Jackson, McLyte, Queen Latifah and Toni Morrison had already showed me that Black girls' social and cultural identities and truths cannot and should not be limited to singular variables.

Exponentiality

Instead, our identities and truths are best described metaphorically in EXPONENTIAL terms. For me, from a research and praxis perspective, exponentiality represents the cosmological and metaphysical possibility of our daughters to grow in ways not necessarily measurable, predictable, or explainable by traditional science.

Then and now, I argued that knowledge of Black girls' ways of knowing, being, and existing in this world requires Multi-vocular, interdisciplinary, transdisciplinary, and dialectical theories, methodologies and pedagogies. Ironically enough, the university library where I attended undergraduate and graduate school, boasted of having the third largest library in the country; Yet, I could not find a hand full of books or articles that taught me about my existence as a Black girl, or about my sisters, mothers, aunts, cousins, god mothers, or neighbors existence living—Black and Girl.

As a psychology major, for instance, I learned that people's behaviors were influenced by cognition and the inability to process information in order to make socially acceptable choices. I rejected much of psychological theory because it was a bunch of dead white men telling women and people of color what is wrong with them as an individual. Abandoning psychology as a major, I then turned to sociology. As a sociology major, I felt like the sociological theories and methodologies of that discipline fit me, like an intellectual glove. But, only like Michael Jackson's Billy Jean glove, and not like that of Janet Jackson's Rhythm Nation glove, hat and boots.

To clarify, sociology felt real good, but almost too good. It was too good at pointing out systematic oppression and institutions' influence on human actions. In my intellectual yearning, I was looking for something more, something that was absent in the sociological imagination; Like Janet's rhythm nation, I was in search of strategies for interrupting power regimes, including regimes of truth. I wanted to know how do people actively resist oppression and dehumanizing conditions, because all my life, growing up on the Southside of Chicago, I witnessed mothers and daughters existing underneath the boots of Black male patriarchy, class oppression, and White supremacy. But, I also witnessed them conscientiously and actively resisting subjugation and terror in our homes, neighborhoods, and schools.

In search of "institutionalized stories of resistance", in other words, those stories that went beyond grandma's kitchen table, I enrolled in women studies and African American history classes. This is where my intellectual troubles began. Through studying other people's stories of oppression and organized resistance, I began to discover my own power and the collective power of my people.

To provide an example of intellectual troubles, I will share a brief story with you all of an undergraduate experience. And, of all the racist and sexist acts that my friends and I encountered on college campuses, this one remains vividly present in my autographical memory.

Political (mis)understandings

In my sophomore year of college, after returning to campus in the month of January, I was too excited to finally have a single room for the first time since leaving for college (actually in life, since I had a sister one year younger than me). I was feeling empowered by my new sense of independence and my new minor, women and gender studies.

So, I came up with the bright idea to decorate my dorm room and door in a way that celebrated me. I decorated the door with big bold pink and purple alphabet letters that read: GIRL POWER! In oversize bubble letters, on the right side of the dorm door was girl power; spelled out with an exclamation mark on the end of the phrase. The White girls living on the residential hall floor lost their proverbial minds!

I became popular overnight. I was no longer invisible on the dorm floor of about 30 girls (I was one of two Black girls on the floor; we were once roommates and attended high school together). Everyone smiled at me; Greeted me by my name, "Hi, Venus. How was your day? By the way, love how you decorated the door." "Oh my god, Venus, Love your hair. Yes, Girl power!" "Venus, you want to go have drinks with us tonight? Go Girls!" With those two words, Girl Power, I had become relevant and visible to those middle class White girls.

However, my popularity ended quicker than it began. February marked Black history month. Again, coming to political consciousness, I decided to decorate my door once again to express myself. This time on the left side of the dorm room door, in the colors red, Black, and green, I hung the words: BLACK POWER! On the right side, vertically hung, were the words, "Girl Power" and on the left, vertically highlighted, "Black Power!" Both with exclamation marks.

Let's just say the White girls lost their minds—again. But, this time residents began to put their heads down and walk right pass me without saying "hello," while others simply shot meet a quick glance accompanied by half-smirks. Soon anonymous letters were placed under my dorm door. Letters informed me that people felt offended by the words Black power, and other letter writers called me a racist. Eventually, the Resident Advisor notified me first verbally, then in writing (as a warning), that Black Power was racist and offensive to other residents and that I needed to take the words down or I would be in violation of resident hall policies that prevented discrimination based on race, gender, sexuality … blah, blah, blah, blah, blah, blah.

To make a long story short, I refused to remove the phrase, "Black Power!", even after being threatened to be forcibly removed from the dorm by police, if necessary. When that threat didn't work, I was asked to educate the girls on the floor about Black power and what it meant to me. I refused. My words went something like this, "I never asked them to teach me about White power, so I will not teach them about Black power." Let's just say that from that day forward, campus police were called when my music was supposedly too loud, when there were too many black bodies in my dorm room, and even when someone "allegedly" smelled pot seeping from underneath my door room door.

Anyhow, I share that story (or those stories) because they provide insight into my early on perspicacity (pur-spi-kas-i-tee) to acknowledge, center, and exercise a Black girl politic. That experience that remains embedded in my psyche begs the questions:

1. What was it about girl power that those college-aged White women viewed as appealing, worth bolstering and celebrating?
2. What was it about Black power that those young White women felt the need to shun, repress, and antagonize?
3. What can be learned from this experience that may help inform current and future education research, theory and praxis?

In brief, isn't it interesting to witness first hand how an adjective can change a conversation and shift the dialogue.

FIELDNOTE 6

VOICE IN RE/PRESENTATION

The researcher's stage

Cultural exchanges

Nanette is a first-generation college student. I first met Nanette after she was hired as a student worker in the department where I worked at the university. Serendipitously, later Nanette was randomly selected as a participant in a study I was conducting on the experiences of Black college-age women (this is an example of how small so-called research sample pools are for students of color on campus, which indicates another limitation of scientific research protocols).

Upon our first encounter, the department was not racially diverse and had not ever had a Black student worker. I remember walking past the main office door with Nanette sitting at the desk. I tried not to look too surprised and shot her a quick glance wearing a smirk on my face; a smile that seemed to convey to her, "Hello. I see you and I'm glad that you are here." It was definitely a cultural exchange that did not need words.

Her returned half smile said, "I'm glad to see you, and I'm glad that you are here."

Soon after seeing Nanette sitting at the student workers' desk in the main office, I bee-lined to my own office. I was giddy for some reason, if not shocked. "Wow, they actually hired a Black student, who actually looked Black?" The day I first saw Nanette she was sporting stylish army type boots, fitted jeans, and a blue jean jacket. Her outfit was certainly celebrating her Black womanish curves and not attempting to hide them in front of the very conservative, small-town White office workers or professors.

On top of her contemporary and stylish outfit, Nanette was also rocking her hair in a mohawk! The girl seriously had style and courage. I wanted to get to know her. I sat down at the desk chair and pretended to arrange items on the desk. Then, I picked up the office phone and called to the front desk. The new student worker picked up. Her voice was very eloquent and professional. She was in character.

"Hello, I am Dr. Evans-Winters. Could you come to my office? I have a quick project in which I need your assistance." I stayed in character.

Nanette, the student worker, was quickly at my door, and she knocked.

"It's open."

At that moment, the student worker stuck her head inside the door. She clearly had "manners" for she chose not to enter until I formally invited her into my space, which was another cultural exchange.

"Come on in."

She was visibly nervous but excited at the same time. Of course, months later, and to this day, we still talk about these sets of first exchanges between us.

"Hi, my name is Dr. Evans-Winters. You can call me Dr. V. What is your name?"

"My name is Nanette," and then, she explained that she was a political science major and African American studies minor.

"Oh, that's an interesting name, like as in, Na-Na. Hahaha. Just kidding." I broke character.

"Actually, people do call me Na-Na." We both giggled. She broke character.

"Na-Na, I need to better organize materials for the class that I'm teaching. Could you please make me a binder with the class name? Thank you."

Nanette left the office in less than five minutes; however, that brief cultural exchange bonded us together for a lifetime. To this day, we joke about how we both pretended like we were not overjoyed to see the other that first day in the office when I spotted Nanette sitting at the student workers' desk. We also joked about how I came up with a bogus project simply to get her alone, so that I could grill her to see if she was legit and a "down" sister. She was legit.

Cultural ethos

Nanette treated me throughout our (cultural) exchanges as an elder (i.e. big sister, auntie, or play mother) while also demonstrating for me, the professor, that she was a professional. Many Black women professors are always *checking out* to see if our Black students remember their *home training*.

Meaning, if a Black student can invoke the ethos of the Black community, while also maintaining an identity that is reflective of what it takes to navigate White academic spaces. I believe for some Black women professors we have high expectations of Black students, especially other Black women college students, in that they are to remain committed to an authentic Black identity, and as a part of that identity, present a confident Black scholarly identity.

Nanette, on that day in my office, demonstrated that she possesses a confident Black scholar identity, an identity that meets at the intersections of Black cultural awareness and knowledge attainment and expression in the interest of the Black community. Interestingly enough, in the first meeting, Nanette was checking me out as well. She wanted to know in her tolerance of my antics, if I was a real down sister or another one of those standoffish, uppity, self-centered kind of Black professors (note: Black professors and students are not one monolithic group. We come to academe with our own research interests, tastes, and personalities. And, all of these ways of existing should be respected). Nanette is not only culturally aware, but also very insightful, and curious. She wanted to know who I was as a professor and as a woman. I believe she was just as intrigued by me as I was with her. We knew we were on a path of learning and supporting each other. Below, excerpted from a larger university study on the experiences of Black college women, are Nanette's storied memories.

Nanette: the flip side of the coin

Excerpt one

Prior to attending college I went to several different schools. I attended about five different elementary schools; I even attended the same one in 3rd and then 8th grade again. My teachers were predominantly black in these schools however being young I didn't understand the importance of that. When I was in high school I would have said that I went to a school that had a lot of black representation, but they did not. There was a selective enrollment test that everyone had to take to get in. The test was early in the morning and there were about 2,000 students there with only a handful of black faces. After the test was over some students began talking about how sleepy they were and how they didn't even finish the test. However, I saw many of these same students at my orientation where I was the only black girl there. There were many black boys who had been recruited to play basketball.

Excerpt two

After not being the model student, and getting into a great amount of trouble I was basically put out of my house and forced to go to college; college wasn't even on my radar … The decision to go to college was made for me. Through a mixture of family court and my family, college was "the way to save my life." I applied to one school and I was accepted. I chose the major Social Work because my best friend, Jalieshia, had chosen that major. Even though my oldest brother was in college I had no aspirations to go myself.

Excerpt three

I began to see all my friends and how excited they were to go to college, and it made me more excited and more interested in going. I began doing more research on the one college that I applied to … I began to see the cost of education; I didn't fully understand how it would all be paid for. I began applying for scholarships. I received three scholarships from the school and one from a Chicago based organization, so with four scholarships plus my financial aid, for the first time I was truly excited to go. I wasn't feeding off someone else's excitement this time, it was truly mine.

Hearing the caged bird sing

One of the biggest challenges has been money to pay for school and money to survive while in school. I left the first university I went to with no transcripts because after four scholarships and my financial aid I was still unable to afford the out of state tuition. I then went to a community college in Chicago to start over completely as a freshman again. By this point I had a strong thirst for knowledge. Coming back I saw the same people in the same place, my "friends" with more children than when I left. It was a place that I knew I eventually wanted to live but not like that. I wanted better for myself.

I never quit. I kept going. At this point I had a very uneducated and less critical view of what being black and being on a white campus meant, being black period. I had always taken pride in being black however it was not until I entered Midwestern University that I was able to fully understand the stance I took on being black and being a woman and standing strongly and firmly in that. This is when my other greatest challenge began: being black and being a woman on this campus.

I think that black women are perceived in two ways on this campus: the angry black woman, or the "black bestie." The angry black women are those in class and on campus who challenges the way things are. I remember walking down the hall while taking a night class. There was a white girl about the same size as me a couple of feet in front of me. She kept looking back and then she began to run. I didn't really think anything of it until I tried to push the bathroom door open and she was up against it pushing it closed screaming at the top of her lungs. I eventually found out that she was in my night class lecture, and because I challenged the professor about calling Emmitt Till by his family nickname "BoBo," she had perceived me as the angry black woman. The "black bestie" is the black girl that white people relate so much to. When they say "my best friend is black" she is the person they are talking about. She is the friend who they relate to because they grew up poor like she did and she doesn't really "remind them of a black person."

Either way once we begin talking our opinions are taken with a grain of salt, what we say doesn't hold as much weight as our white counterparts or men. Either way we are perceived as weak and inferior. I felt a constant struggle to assert ourselves amongst the black women that I worked with. I almost felt like a joke in my classes and when I had to do certain things in front of university officials. On two occasions my Black History Month Cultural Dinner speech was changed because the housing department (they hosted the cultural dinners) did not want to offend the majority. I was confused as to how asserting blackness at a Black Cultural Dinner could offend anyone. On the other hand, I have met several black women on campus who tell me that racism, classism, elitism, and several other "-isms" are not an issue in this day and age.

....

Yes, I do believe my experiences are similar to other students attending the university. For example, when an organization wants money to bring a speaker or put on a program they go to the funding board, a board of about 9 students, which always seem to be all white students, and propose for the money. The general rule of the funding board is that at least 50% of the student population would want to attend this program. When you are proposing money for a black speaker to come and black people make up less that 5% of the student population you already have the odds stacked against you walking into the meeting. So you change the goal and integrity of your program to get money to host it.

So many black organizations I am familiar with and have worked with go in front of this board and try to appeal to white students but when so many organizations get money for programs that don't appeal to students of color we begin the critical discussions. Many black women on this campus experience some of the same things I have experienced. From being accused of stealing out of a white group member's purse in class to being asked to speak for the entire black population when you are the only black person in class. It is very hard to be black on this campus without being labeled in a negative way, especially when the word "ghetto" is thrown around like an adjective, when some don't understand that the use of the word "nigger" to describe black people isn't ok.

....

I think that my biggest support at the university came in the form of black women friends who were conscious. I was able to have open conversations and express myself without being called "too sensitive" or "angry." I then found mentors in two women in the department I worked in. I had never met women like them in my life. Although I had a general idea about what I was doing in life I was not set on a path until I met them. I was challenged in my thought process in such a productive way that I appreciated. I was treated with love and tough love. I had people who would advise me on situations and encouraged me to do what I thought was best. I then thought it was best to not "hog" these women, that I should share them with women of color on campus who needed this type of thought and personality in their lives. We had black women who worked on campus who helped us but nothing as productive as these two women alone. One of my friends and I were considered leaders in the black woman population on campus however there was so much that we couldn't help with, and needed help with ourselves that we needed these women. We needed them like our very lives depended on it. I don't think they will ever know what the presence did and still does for me and other women of color on campus.

....

I would say to young women be yourself and love yourself. Never take your eyes off what you came to do and above all stay hungry! Stay with a hunger for all things. Whether it's justice, education, love, life, or experience, stay hungry! The bare minimum will never be enough for you. Never feel that as women you are not good enough because institutions will try to make you feel that way. One of your goals should be being a voice for women, realizing that there is something bigger than you that you have to contribute to.

Building relationships with women is one of the most important things I did in college. Build relationships with women! Other women will be your greatest allies, not saying you have to be "besties" with every black woman you see! Realize that lighting someone else's candle does not necessarily take away from your flame! A quote that I have on my desk and read every day is one that sums this all up:

"African women in general need to know that it's OK for them to be the way they are—to see the way they are as a strength, and to be liberated from fear and silence"— Wangari Maathai. Don't be scared or silent when it comes to being a woman, whether you are a woman of color or not, silence or fear will not protect you.

The researcher's voice

Epilogue

Nanette frequently reminds me, "I grew up on the west side, in the projects. My mama still lives in the projects." Chicago, where Nanette and I both hail and the city that we both love, unfortunately, has gained a national reputation for its violence. Nanette, like many young Black women going off to college have had to endure and cope with growing up in some of Chicago's roughest ghettoized neighborhoods (I use this term to refer to the social construction of urban Black communities, due to intentional economic disinvestment, racial segregation, school closures, and political bargains). Not much is known about how Black young women cope with the sedimentation of inequality.

The university community where the ethnography took place recruits students from Chicago's "south side," "west side," and collar suburbs, which are all predominately Black. Nanette would have been born and matriculated through schooling right in the middle of the windy city's most calamitous times for Blacks, especially the city's lower-income and working-class residents—the early 1990s and 2000s.

What has people so alarmed here is the rapid increase in the number of gang-related killings, especially drive-by shootings in which innocent bystanders sometimes are hit. From June, 1989 to May, 1990, Chicago had 334 drive-by shootings.

~Los Angeles Times, June 23, 1990

The year marked the greatest number of slayings with guns since 1974, when the city recorded its highest murder toll ever, 970 slayings, 669 with guns. There were 433 gun murders in 1989. Killings with guns have increased almost 60 percent since 1985, to 602 from 378.

~Chicago Tribune, January 02, 1991

Since January 1, 1990, an astonishing 14,919 people have been murdered in Chicago. Even worse, many of the victims have been children.

~Examiner.com, October 30, 2012

Shootings over the Memorial Day weekend left seven people dead and another 45 wounded in Chicago ... The violence this weekend was similar to three of the last five Memorial Day weekends: 53 gunshot victims in 2012, and 58 in 2015. A total of 34 people were shot in 2014, and 21 were shot in 2013.

~Chicago Tribune, May 30, 2017.

The above are excerpted headlines and quotes from newspaper reports on crime in Chicago. There is no doubt that many of us who survived the early 1990s to mid- 2000s went to college carrying hurt and pain as a result of witnessing close up and personal drug trafficking, drug addiction, gun violence, and police brutality. What we did not understand is just how much of the city's Black residents' struggle with mental health issues, drug addiction, homelessness, poverty, and poor quality schooling was directly related to the city's political and economic neglect of its Black residence. For many, the college years simply perpetuated and cemented the racism, sexism, and classism that permeates throughout the city. Yet, there are intentional ways that knowledge and resilience can transform one's personal and collective power. We strive to recollect such power and resilience through the research and pedagogical process.

FIELDNOTE 7

WRITING MY DAUGHTER'S BODY

In the episodes below, I attempt to articulate my internal struggle with research *on* young people. An episode is an incident in the course of a series of events, in a person's life or experience, or an incident or scene within a narrative. From a psychological perspective, an episode may also represent a distinctive period in an individual's life that includes a heightened (psychosomatic) mood, usually abnormal (e.g. depressive, irritation, fear, anger, etc.). Below, we witness my various internal selves in a conversation, regarding my daughter's presence in my service work with West African girls representing various ethnic/tribal affiliations.

The voice of my *academic self* represents my formal training as a scholar, researcher, and pedagogue. Whereas *cultural reflections* are representative of the cultural understandings that one brings to her ethnographic contexts and pedagogical endeavors. Cultural reflections here represent my own internalized beliefs, morals, and values that I borrow from my primary culture(s). Most qualitative researchers are taught to be cognizant of their own cultures and how it influences the research process.

Lastly, I engage in *mother speak*. Mother speak represents for me an intuition—or internal voice—derived from socialization (to play my role as a girl, woman, and child), formal learning (e.g. reading books, stories, and other texts on parenting and child development), and biological instinct. At any moment in the field, these multiples selves, multiple voices are sometimes in conflict while at other times incongruence.

Episode I

I had been traveling back and forth to the continent of Africa since 2008. Traveling with a team of education researchers and practitioners, I believe that I only experienced the elite side of South Africa. A year later I returned on my own to volunteer in the field of social work, providing therapy services and job skill preparation in a high poverty, high density HIV/AIDS township. The child rape rate was a challenge for mothers, social workers, and police. I hope I was somewhat of an intervening factor with my formal education. I know education, and I know social work; and I know I have inside knowledge into girls as well as aspects of African ways of being.

......

Despite always having to be aware of my surroundings, I was more comfortable in South Africa than I was at home. There I was free from drowning in Whiteness, and safe from suffocating at the hands of White supremacy. I was an outsider, but at least I had the privilege of privilege (i.e. American status, educated, English-speaking, middle class, lighter-skin, loose hair texture, adornments, etc.). However, the heaviness of poverty overwhelmed me; it was like being back on the Southside of Chicago. Only here in South Africa, I had less knowledge of the culture. Here I had social capital but no cultural wealth. After two years of serving in South Africa, I jumped on a plane and went to volunteer in Ghana. Ghana felt like home. Ubuntu.

....

My African princess is now nine. I have been traveling abroad alone since she was four. She never knew to miss me. However, now she is older and interested in what I do. She wants to be me. Yet, at nine, I see too that she is becoming more independent—stubborn and sassy. I acknowledge that she is transitioning to becoming a strong-minded Black woman ... but too soon. She ain't earned it. I decide to take her with me. Let her see how hard other girls work, and how they maintain, as a part of their womanhood, a sense of humility and respect for their elders. She's ecstatic for such a responsible experience. I'm thinking discipline. She's thinking contact with a different culture. Either way, there would be expectations for her or norms that she would learn to navigate. When packing for her, I noticed American clothes sexualize little girls. I won't pack any capris, sleeveless shirts, short-shorts, or leggings. She would only get the basics. Do I pack in the suitcase four weeks' worth of clothes? No, I only pack five days' worth of clothes.

Episode II

I have engaged with aspects of African culture, South Africa and West Ghanaian culture in particular, for nearly ten years. I decide to submit an IRB proposal to study my teaching experiences in Ghana with rural girls. This would be my third year teaching "English as an Academic Language" and "Girls Leadership and Empowerment."

The purpose of this study is look at my own pedagogical practices working with rural school girls ... The study serves the purpose of understanding what it means to teach students who are culturally different from the teacher, and should inform more about teaching across differences. The study could help us understand more about teacher development and multiculturalism.

~IRB research protocol excerpt, 2015

For the record, while teaching ("in the field"), I withdrew the IRB proposal. In my opinion, based on my observations (or unintentional study of myself studying my daughter), I realized the entire "project" was unethical. Truthfully, I began to question how I wrote about and depicted images of African-born girls, since I was reluctant and hesitant to discuss intimate moments that myself and my own (biological) daughter shared.

......

In Ghana, I have 30 daughters; 31 if I include the one that I birthed. I was responsible for the 30 girls in the camp, my biological daughter, and even the neighbor's children. I was trusted because I too was raising a Black girl. I found myself feeding other people's daughters; braiding and beading a neighbor's daughter's hair; and even having to discipline the teen girls as if they were my own. In return, they cared for me hand-and-foot. Girls carried my belongings, prepared my bath water, prepared and served me food, and watched my daughter like their own little sister or child.

Where were the ethical and moral boundaries discussed in the IRB? There were no boundaries. As a teacher/mother/elder/auntie in Ghana, I was expected to scream, cuss, and hit if necessary. That's where I drew the boundaries. I am a teacher who does not hit.

But, we twerked, popped, rolled, and dropped it … and even my daughter and I learned Azonto. Might I add to a near science? We not only danced together but we dressed, prayed, and bathed together. I'm not here for the science of it, but because this culture is my metaphorical water.

......

My daughter has gone "native." She has definitely become more humble. She understands her role as a girl/woman-child. She is being taught about the culture from a girl's perspective. Not a Black perspective, but a Black African girl perspective. Gender matters. She is taught, no told, what it is that girls are supposed to do. She takes care of younger children, she is required to help cook, she must wash the laundry—by hand—and, it is her job to "fetch" water; and, she now fetches water without being told and carries the bucket on her head. And she is left at the compound with other children, and watched by the elders and aunties nearby, and even sent to the market to retrieve some needed item.

Relieving herself in the bush is more convenient (or fun) than a requirement. As a teacher, she teaches about American culture. As a student, she learns about hygiene in Ghana, STDs, and diseases like malaria, menstruation, child marriage, child labor, and teen pregnancy. She learns of the women's bucket and the men's bucket. She learns that at certain times of the month, women aren't allowed to share a bucket with the men. She and I for the first time in our life share the same non-flushable toilet; mind you, she's in charge of dumping the bathroom garbage. She has gained culturally relevant skills as well as knowledge about sexual and biological health. She also learned that animals, insects, and dirt were a part of our natural habitat. My daughter has learned that girls and women are both strong and vulnerable and able.

By week four, she is beginning to ask me and her village and city aunties, "Why do the girls refer to me as White?" We try to explain that the girls are looking at her brown skin, light colored eyes, hair texture, speech, and "fancy" clothes to figure out their own (mis)understandings about racial, tribal/ethnic, and national affiliation. "Daughter, they aren't questioning if you are a Black person, they are questioning your 'sameness' as them." Your Americanness. Soon enough, she began to challenge her fellow classmates/students/sisters directly.

"Why do ya'll call me White? I am not White! I am Black, I am African."

Giggles and embarrassment from her peers.

Then, "But, Sister Serena, you have light-skin."

Armed Serena fires back, "But, sister Ama is lighter than me!"

More giggles.

"Serena, but your hair."

Long hair adorned with beads, and hair worn out and exposed as a school-age girl is practically taboo. All her peers' hair was worn very low, in a ball fade cut; similar to how Black boys wear their hair in the U.S. Serena also wore long earrings (designed in the girls' art class) and bright-colored clothes that she sported to class every day.

"Is my mom Black African?"

"Yes!" with head nods.

Hands raise.

"Sister Serena (her name is usually drawn out when spoken, emphasis on reeen-naa), you speak very fast. Your English is fancy."

Everyone claps.

Finally, Serena was out'ed because of her fanciness. As expected, Serena exuded middle class-ness. It was partially my fault, because once I realized that I was "policing her body," which is against my feminist leanings, I let her adorn earrings, necklaces, and the type of clothes she felt comfortable. She liked expressing her fanciness.

Episode III

As a formally trained social worker, I understand the significance of sexual harassment, teen pregnancy, and child marriage on a girl's self-esteem, reproductive health, safety, and future education and economic opportunities. In rural communities, girls from poor families are particularly vulnerable to child sexual abuse and forced early marriage. Drawing from my social work background and teaching background, at the girls' camp, I am in a unique position to align discussions on reproductive health to youth-centered and girl-empowering curriculum.

For instance, I watched in awe as I saw aunties (older women) use stories and metaphors to teach about girls' health. In a deep, but soft voice, and in Ghanaian English, Professor Nana explained to the girls, "When you begin to go through your changes, you are a ripe fruit. Men look at you, like fruit hanging from the tree. They see right away how supple you are. They want to taste you. They want to take the fruit and enjoy its ripeness. Suckle at the nectar."

Our elder teacher continued, "They will try to whisper in your ear, say nice things to you, give you gifts to make you feel special. They only do-ing it to taste your juiciness. But, it is up to you not to fall for it." The girls giggled softly and shyly. I squirmed in my seat and smiled stupidly. I was not feeling the metaphor, but I appreciated the metaphor. I appreciated the candor, but I did not want to accept male innocence, or that girls had that much control over their bodies. I pondered for days afterwards, how do we respect culture while also using scientific-based knowledge to educate girls on sexual reproductive health and the realities of child rape and sexual abuse? I looked toward the back of the class, across thirty other girls, to find my own daughter. As we caught eye contact, I knew that she understood that her body will soon be ripening too. Professor Nana's story was easier for her to understand puberty than my explanations of periods, public hair, and breasts. TMI. The American way.

......

I grew up in a community where sexual harassment was all too common. Black girls looked on us our mothers were whistled out and talked at by male on-lookers on the street. One of my earliest memories is of a man screaming to my mother while she walked by, "Hey, now, do fries come with the shake?" as he looked as her ass passed by. By the time I was in middle school, it was commonplace for boys to get "free feels" on the playground and touch girls' budding breasts and buttocks. Also, most girls in the neighborhood had experienced sexual harassment from strangers. Several times, I have witnessed women assaulted simply waiting on the bus stop, or called a bitch for not responding to a man's requests for attention, a name, or a phone number. Once I was groped while walking near the beach, at night, with a group of my friends. The gang of boys ran pass our gender-mixed group so quickly that more than likely their intent for being in that space was simply to intimidate and harass the public. Swiftly the dude rubbed my vaginal area with his hand. Luckily, I wore jeans that evening that served as a barrier to my private part, but I still felt violated. Raped. And, I was thinking why me? I guess it was easier to harass my small frame than one of the boys in the group. By the time high school came and went, most of us girls were used to unwanted advances from strangers, friends and family alike. Much of this wanted and unwanted attention from boys and men left many of my peers vulnerable and (victims?) of early pregnancy.

My own experiences as a Black girl growing up in working class and poor neighborhoods helped me connect with the experiences of adolescent African girls.

......

I am used to stares or second glances. My big afro is a rarity in Ghana. It doesn't help that it is colored sun-kissed orange. Also, I wear a lot of jewelry, like bangle bracelets and big Bahamadia earrings. I was told by a 20-something Ghanaian brother that Ghana women do not wear so much jewelry. There goes that myth. However, I was surprised at the extra-long glances that my daughter received. But, I have come to understand that her bright colored clothes, designer shoes, earrings, hair beads, light eyes, and caramel skin complexion helped her to stand out. She would get compliments from strangers similar to the way most children do in the States. Ghanaian children come in all shapes, sizes, and colors. I believe people were reading her class. And, of course her education, when she opened her mouth and English flowed out so easily.

As I prepared her for travel to the village to visit my two-year-old Godson and his family, I dressed her up and packed her in comfortable and more worn clothes. I did not want us to stand out too much. When we arrived to the bus depot, we already stood out. The "depot" can best be described as a market full of unlicensed drivers bidding for travelers. Most of them do not speak English, and speak in a variety of tongues or dialects. My friend had to negotiate the price for us both my daughter and I to go on the van. In Twi, she explained to the driver that we needed seats for two, where we would be traveling to, we were not familiar with the land and that we did not speak the language. Therefore, we needed to be told about rest stops, when to get off, and where to go once we came to our final destination. We gave the driver money for the cost of the seat, plus another cedi for accommodating our lack of knowledge. I later learned the driver's English was not good at all. He signed to me, used hand signals. Luckily, a mother or sister would usually tell me what was going on during the trip.

We boarded the van. The passenger van is designed to sit eleven. Like in the Ghana way, there were fourteen travelers. One infant, three children, and ten adults. Although I paid for two seats, I got more like a 1 ½ seat. My daughter sat somewhat on and off my lap. Her booty was getting bigger. My right thigh was numb. I propped my legs on my backpack on the floor, and my daughter sat her smaller backpack in her lap. The travel time was five hours, with no air-conditioning or toilets; driving across bumpy, rocky, mostly unpaved roads. I listened to the passengers complain that the government was "taking all these taxes, but not giving us roads."

One woman began a lone discussion about government immorality. That's is all that I could translate and decipher of the conversation. I have taken this trip several times without my daughter, and I would usually enjoy music blaring through my ear buds. But, while traveling with my daughter, I had to entertain her and listen out for any confusion. I was on mother alert.

An hour into to the trip, a man sitting next to my daughter begins to look back and forth between me and my daughter, while speaking Ewe. He was talking to all in the van clearly. My daughter was at ease. I was on guard. He was intentionally speaking Ewe to see if I understood what he was saying to the woman next to him. The woman next to him laughed playfully.

Finally, he turned to me and said, "You no understand Ewe?" In a friendly tone, I responded that I did not know Ewe. He turned to the woman next to him, and began to speak to her in Twi. Next, he turned, looked at my daughter, and then looked at me. I asked him in English, "What did you say about my daughter?" A few passengers laughed. The man responded surprisingly, "Ohhhh, you speak Twi?"

"No, I don't speak Twi very well," pointing to my ear, "I can understand some words when I hear it."

He explained, "I was saying how beautiful your daughter is. How old is she?"

"Tell him Serena."

"I am nine."

"You are pretty."

"Thank you."

Now, my daughter is tickled to death, but I read that she is also nervous. She scoots closer to me, but there is nowhere to go, but fully on my lap. I think to myself it is not possible for me to sit her fully on my lap without one, offending him if he was only being playful; two, sweating to death and risking dying of heat exhaustion; three, bursting my urine-filled bladder; or four being smashed to death by her new found weighty behind. She was no longer a baby. I was no longer strong enough to carry her.

I wrapped my right arm slightly around her shoulder (oh, my god, it's too hot to be touching another human being) to let her know that I could feel her discomfort. However, my urban girl mothering instinct told me to use this as a teaching moment. The lesson: Honey, sometimes shit is out of our control as women, and we must be stern and strong, even when we feel like withering away. She did not wither away physically or emotionally, but she refused to doze off to sleep.

The man looked at my daughter and says playfully, "Would you be my wife? You could be my second wife." He then turns to the woman next to him, and says to me, "My wife says it is okay. She can be my second wife." The van is quiet. The wife laughs nervously.

"She is nine. I am sure that her father would not like that." Yes, I pulled the patriarchy card. My daughter did not wither away physically or emotionally, but she refused to doze off to sleep.

Not much later the van came to a halt. One of the grandmothers needed a urine break after an hour and a half into the trip. The man jumped out to take a piss behind the van while the women went off to the bushes. At that time, I crossed my daughter over my lap to exchange seats. She held both backpacks in her lap to accommodate the new seating arrangement. Poor baby. She now sat to my left, and her thighs touched an elder woman's thigh. I relaxed my legs and let my big ass and thighs take up more space than I really needed. The intent was to put distance between my daughter and the over age male admirer. Even if that distance was more imaginary than real. After finishing his business and having a cigarette, the man scooted back into the van next to me.

His next and last words to us were, "Goodbye." My daughter shot him a fake smile. The smile where she only shows her top row of teeth. I shot him a fake smile. The one where only my top front row of teeth are showing.

In Twi, "Mah krow," politely rolls off my tongue. Daughter and I do not know whether we are flattered or insulted in the moment. We knew we were adventurous warriors in that moment. A team.

Epilogue

After the van episode, my daughter had two more "marriage proposals." Again, we do not know to this day how serious the advances were; all that we do know is that the boldness of the men became less flattering and more offensive for us both. My daughter learned to turn away and look at me without a smile, but with stern look of defiance. Not turn away out of fear, but sending the message through her body and unspoken words that she would not entertain the matters of adults. Marriage was a topic for adults. Further, my daughter turned her body to me, as a silent act of protest. I taught her if a man or older boy approached her when I was not around to ignore them, or "be firm" and "use her assertive voice."

We practiced, "My mom does not allow me to play with adults" and "I have to ask my mom." Fortunately, my daughter reports not having any issues with advances or male attention when I was not present. In my mind, I knew that I was indirectly socializing her into Black girlhood. There is a code of silence. The silence is that we do not talk about the internalized fear that we have when Black mothers allow our daughters to become more independent despite us knowing that there is a risk of our daughters' innocence being subtly or overtly being accosted by male attention.

Many Black mothers flashback to our own childhood when our mothers left us behind with someone she trusted, or maybe not trusted and went against her own instinct, and we became easily accessible victims. The scenes below reminded me of the seriousness of child brides and the vulnerability of girl children all over the world.

Scene I: (Inside a friend's home in the village).

My friend woke up sick. She vomited and cried, and bent over with pain in her stomach area. We shared a room, sleeping on separate mattresses on the floor. My daughter shared a mattress with me. I told my friend that her symptoms were not normal and that we needed to get her to a hospital. Her two-year-old nursing son began to scream out—afraid for his mother. We summoned for our friend to go into town to find a taxi. Once the taxi arrived, I informed my daughter and another 12-year-old girl in the house, Patience, to stay with the little child and to take care of their chores (e.g. breakfast, bathe the toddler, and fetch water). Also, in the house was a 17-year-old houseboy who could watch over them while we were away.

Approximately five hours later I returned to the house via motorcycle. I was scared and exhausted at the hospital, for in those five hours, I was trapped in a hospital with no running water, overcrowded rooms, and no ventilation. Even worse, I was in a hospital room with five patients cramped together with no privacy, some vomiting and coughing. In fact, someone died right in front of me, and his body just laid there, until a nurse came to cover the body. I started to have an anxiety attack before I had enough sense to get fresh air on a bench in the courtyard outside the one level hospital. Hospital personnel were asking me questions that I could not answer, and most times, I could not translate.

Finally, an American trained doctor spoke English to me and explained the medical diagnoses and treatment to occur. He said that I could leave, but I should arrange for someone to bring food for dinner and breakfast, nightclothes, and bedding for my friend. I arranged for "Auntie" in the compound to bring everything the doctor ordered.

As I sat on the family couch in the den, I debriefed neighbors and friends of the situation. I even spoke with family members from villages deeper in the bush. I understood two phrases, "Thank you" and "God bless you, sistah." Gathered around eating food prepared for us by a neighboring auntie, the 17-year-old boy begins to speak.

He says, "Mama (referring to me), I want Serena to be my third wife. She must be my third wife, because you know I have my future wife, my girlfriend. Patience will be my second wife."

Before I could say a word, our male friend, 20-year-old something C.K. began to scream in a thick Ghanaian accent, "You muthafucka! You fuckin' sick bastard! You should neva be in this house. You are a fuckin' pervert. I should beat yo' ass." The two young men were already at odds, because the older one did not believe that a younger man should be living in the house with a single woman and two underage children. He thought the young man's presence would confuse the toddler, thinking he was his father. However, our friend as a single woman felt that she could use the help of the boy around the house as he adjusted to being away from his more rural home village in order to find work to pay for school.

The teen began to nervously giggle. And, he utters some kind of excuse to explain what he was trying to convey. However, exhausted and tired of trying to "stay in my place" as a woman and cultural outsider, but very well aware of my "mama" status, I chime in, "If I even catch you looking at any one of those girls, I will beat your ass myself." He left the room in shame.

I spent the rest of the night beating myself up, because I could not stop thinking to myself what could have happened to those girls. I thought about the times the girls had to walk around in wraps after bathing, or the times they had to stay home for chores while we went out or enjoyed leisure time, adult time, while the adolescent girls stayed behind at night. I could not stop thinking about how older boys may groom girls for years before propositioning a girl. I could not help but think about how many poor girls are wooed by older boys who could promise them something that their families could not provide, like money, their own beds, less chores, and even attention.

Scene II (Bus depot in town)

C.K. (who intimately refer to himself as my son) rushes my daughter and me through the market area where all the vans and cars await and bid for passengers. Due to the absence of public transportation and the lack of affordability of cars, the market area is an easy way for unemployed men to make money. The problem is that there is not enough transportation for everyone to get to and from the city. As an outsider, it would very difficult for me to tell a driver where I am going and to bargain my price. Besides, I could be taken advantage of by shady drivers, out-bid, or risk my words being lost in translation.

Once C.K. arranged for Serena and me to have two "comfortable" seats (I needed a window and daughter certainly would not sit by herself or in the luggage area. Period.), we stood close to van as more passengers bargained. We did not want our seats sold. Also, the ethnographer in me enjoyed people watching. I loved the rhythm of sounds that I could not understand. I appreciated the warm smiles and questions inquiring, "Who is the little girl?" Ironically, in the village, my daughter was the exotic other. Other little girls walked up to her, "Water?" We purchased the water from the market girls. They could not be more than nine or ten themselves. Were they lingering because they thought we had money, or did they want to talk with Serena? As the van began to fill with makeshift storage bags (e.g. garbage bags, pillow cases, airport size travel bags, etc.), all the passengers began to stock up for our ride back to the city or villages along the way. Smoke fish for sell, boiled eggs for sell, corn and bread for sell. Bush meat came later down the road.

My daughter was only allowed to drink sealed water from the bag (government approved) and food that I handed her personally. She understood about food safety issues in the country. Our traveling medical doctor informed her the seriousness of food born bacteria that could invade her foreign body more easily than local residents' adapted systems, and she learned in the girls' summer camp of the lack of education on hygiene and food preparation of street vendors. She understood that she could get sick and experience vomiting, diarrhea, constipation, or worse, cholera, typhoid fever, or food poisoning.

My daughter was taught that these symptoms occur due to lack of access to safe clean water to prepare food and wash one's hands. Thus, she always shook her head no to the girl sellers, in a way that indicated, "I want to help you out, but I can't."

It was time to take our place on the bus, before we lost our seats. Yet, when I went to hug and say goodbye to C.K., a young man quickly came in between us. And, with us back turned toward me, he began to say something that I could not understand. And, this time I did not have the privilege of reading his lips or facial expression.

When he stepped aside, and looked back and forth between my daughter and me, I can tell by the expression on C.K. face that something rubbed him the wrong way. He was shaking his head, "no," while looking at the ground. Mumbled something else. I witnessed C.K. wave him off with a gesture of the hand. A wave that is common in Ghanaian culture to indicate that someone is through listening to the speaker, and the person is not worthy of their time. C.K. appeared irritated. Or, was it frustration. Embarrassment? The young man looked me up and down, said something quickly to C.K., and walked away swiftly. My Black girl instinct kicked in and I could not understand why C.K. was not making eye contact with the young man. Is not that what men do to show respect and not fear? C.K. caught me reading him and the situation.

"He asked me if Serena could be his wife. I told him that she was too young."

C.K. continued, "Do you not see her mother?" Then C.K. explains, "He said that you were too old."

Daughter and I laughed.

A mama prayed for safe travels and we departed the village. Due to a road being closed, being beyond immediate repair, the van had to cross the river to the other side on a trolley. A trip that would take two hours in the States, and was typically five hours in Ghana, now became six hours. My time was spent teaching an eight-year-old boy how to play Candy Crush. He did not have the finger dexterity to master the game. My daughter people watched. I shared my daughter's U.S. bought fruit snacks with the child. Mama and aunties sang Christian songs to pass the time. We were stopped by the police.

Exercising my American-ness and English and femininity, I inquired from the handsome police officers why we were stopped. One dark chocolate handsome officer responded, "Child traffickers. Children are not permitted to be stowed without a parent." I nodded my head. Then, I thought to myself, "So, that's why they took the unaccompanied underage girl from the storage area of the van and sat her on the lap of an old lady to pretend that was her child." Was that a little girl who had to get to a family member in another village or a soon to be child laborer or trafficked girl? "Goodbye officer."

"Enjoy your stay in Ghana, sister."

At the next urine break, I purchased food from a street vendor girl. Two cedis. My daughter enjoyed smoke fish, the little boy and girl enjoyed their yams. The little girl exited the van and the stranger's lap excitedly. She ran across the road and jumped in the arms of a young woman who looked elated to embrace the girl.

My daughter and I both sat back in silence for at least two more hours, during the ride, not exchanging any words. We were in peace.

Aligning my mother spirit with the ethnographic gaze

In the pursuit of self-determination, Black women have relied on creative and alternative ways of producing and validating knowledge and of naming and identifying our experiences. Taking on a dialogical voice in the design and pursuit of knowledge is a result of Black women's experiences in communal and civic spaces (Collins, 2002). Consequently, it is common for those who take on a Black feminist stance to use personal narratives, to share personal conversations or symbols and metaphors as a way to convey information or to question the validity of knowledge claims (Dillard, 2000). In the above, I attempt to reveal my shared experiences with my daughter as a cultural insider-outsider. I write about the tensions that occur across my multiple identities and selves.

In the discussion, I also seek to blur the dichotomy between rationality and emotionality. In particular, I cannot ignore my *academic self*. Academic training and socialization facilitates an urge to name, categorize and explain taken-for-granted decisions made in everyday social interactions. To be able to explain the academic self in textual analysis can help organize and make linear often very complex ideas and exchanges.

Similarly, throughout my ethnographic ponderings, I draw upon cultural knowledge. My *cultural selves* permit me to engage cultural contexts based on my knowledge of local norms, symbols, artifacts, forms of speech, rituals and traditions. Of course, these cultural selves are informed by my negotiations of ascribed gender, race, and class expectations and norms. Through a cultural lens, dialogical exchanges, human interactions, and other tangible and intangible items in the environment become cultural cues open for interpretation. Cultural cues become an asset to cultural insiders, and, thus, are very significant in knowledge formation.

In the above dialogue, my *mother voice* presents itself as well throughout the discussion. For me, how I parent is informed by cultural upbringing and under-standings as well an academic skill set (e.g. empirical and theoretical knowledge on child development, gender socialization, racial identity formation, etc.). Although cultural socialization may have taught me to protect my children by any means necessary, no textbook has provided any explanation to the role that kinship, instinct, or spiritual connectedness plays in urges to defend my daughter's body and psyche from real or perceived threats.

As an "other mother" to many daughters, I have a responsibility to meet many girls' and young women's basic needs (e.g. feed, clothe, shelter, and provide financial support) and help teach them how to navigate their social environment. Giving attention to this biological, cultural, and spiritual phenomenon called "mothering" is worth serious investigation. How can "mothering" inform the research process? A multiple consciousness portrayed above brings forth alternative viewpoints on the ethics of care in our pursuits of truth(s). Below, I discuss in detail my own interpretations of the episodic tales above.

A note of dialogical voice(s)

Standing in my mother, sister-girl Black woman truth, I am not comfortable with sharing the specifics of my daughter's and my experiences together. Thus, is it rea-sonable to believe that other mothers of daughters also desire some level of protection of their daughters' public, yet, private experiences with life? I realized during the process of reflecting on my daughter's experiences "in the field" that I was always talking theory, and that I failed to deeply reflect upon the seriousness and urgency of street harassment, teen pregnancy, and child brides in the African context.

As an ethnographer, I was trained to document and "jot down," "memo," and provide "thick description" and "snapshots" of my field experiences. However, after introducing my own daughter into "the field site," I began to question how I wrote about and depicted images of African girls and youth. If I felt hesitance in sharing images of my own daughter in academic and public spaces, then why would I share images and stories of other girls' vulnerabilities? From the multiple voices exercised above, and various episodes, I want to intentionally problematize the idea of researchers representing youth voices and experiences.

I want to raise the question, "Can we fully represent young women's humanity, vulnerability, and agency?" I also wish to ponder the following: Are the social actors themselves (parents, daughters, youth, etc.) truly able to comprehend what exactly they are giving us researchers permission to do with their stories? Do they truly understand what it means to have someone outside of their cultural context (and being) represent them? What are the ethical and moral dilemmas to attempting to represent another human being in writing?

These questions I believe can be answered through my experience writing and depicting the experience of my own daughter. Personally, I do not believe that everything that a young girl experiences should be written about. Some of those experiences are hers alone to experience and decide if they should be shared when she is more aware of herself and the social world. Second, I believe that social experience often takes years of lived experience to decipher, and should be deciphered from multiple perspectives. Lastly, I believe that no human being (or in our case researcher) can justify their right to tell someone else's story. There seems to be more magic in telling one's own story as it takes place alongside other characters in their stories.

Note of emphasis: My daughter gave permission to share her experiences in writing and conference presentations. Many of her experiences during the time the above episodes took place were omitted out of respect for her privacy and dignity as well as my own privacy as her mother. As she ages, and she wishes to share her stories from the motherland learning and teaching alongside West African rural village girls, then she can inscribe her own *daughtering* experiences, body and cultural politics for public consumption.

FIELDNOTE 8

UNVEILING THE MASK (OF TONI)

Masks

Why do I feel like this?

Sometimes I just wish I could take a pill for this and that it could go away.

I try hard

So hard every day not to walk around showing my wounds

So I cover them.

See I'm a master of disguise,

Every smile, laugh, wink, giggle, dance, prance, or glance as of recently as meant nothing to me

Just a way for no one to catch on to me.

It's like robbing a bank, you disguise your face so that no one knows, no one can find your true identity

Just whom you seem to be

I wonder how happiness would feel if it found out that I was taking from it unjustly.

I wonder would it send sadness or anger, to find me

And bind and tie me up or cuff me and then place real feelings inside of me

But I don't know what the fuck those are

I just know that the shit hurts

I just know that at the drop of dime I cry because shit I stole so much from happiness

See those masses of mask kits

They caught my ass and took back they shit

So I'm just left empty

Waiting for a release, I stopped praying a long time ago because I gave up on that God being able to hear me.

Yea I know that Job had his trials before the end of the tunnel, but it doesn't mean he felt good about that shit

****

So where do I find my release, so I thought I would be happy in the black community.

I thought things like these open mics,

Had immunity from all the fake ass rapper wannas,

These I am MC, but only when you see me at open mics,

Because I had to leave for the weekend to make sure that my nails, weaves and Nikes, Jordans or whomever the fuck had they name of the side of my shows was tight

I thought I had immunity from all these catty as bitches

The snitches

O not really snitches, but I meant twitter gangtas

Who think that get some fucking hegemony for making a fucking glorified image of themselves and Dr. Phil I help the fucking community wanna-bes

Sorry but You ain't shit

See I thought I had immunity from all the hypocritical motherfuckers lurking in these fucking churches,

Who tell me how too little my motherfucking skirts is,

And say real womyn don't wear leggings, without checking how big their shirts is

Condemning me, because obviously I didn't find where the right Bible verse is

That would show me how to act like a real womyn

I apologize, but I will always embrace these chocolate brown thighs, ass, tits and the many other gods gifts that he bestows upon me because I was blessed that he equipped me with a brain as well

I thought, I thought, men were the fucking answer

I wondered, why can't I long to get a piece of their ass and thighs

Hyper-sexualize and exploit them

Why must I must be crucified when all I wanted to do was nut or two,

or multiple times if he was up to the challenge

but I digress

But I thought I was immune from my family.

Who back these motherfuckers cracked

And beat until I didn't have much more of any piece of me left

They still came from right and left

Begging, nagging, bitching, complaining, and whining about how fucking hard the world was

And thought since I was well off

I wouldn't mind

Having them in mind when they wanted to spend my dime

So what I am left with nothing, but fucking battle scars and damaged masks in masses

Because I have to put on so many faces that I can't find wear what my true mask is

Well I guess I do know what it is

It is clinically known as depression.

And the fucked up thing about it is

It's the hardest fucking mask to take off your face

~Mask, by Toni

Toni: a commentary on school life from behind the mask

I was a pretty successful student in elementary school. I felt that I had a supportive home environment and loved being around my family. Although the school I attended was by no means the best school in the area at all, I still did what I could to avoid falling into the pitfalls that causes most students not to graduate. In my neighborhood it is likely that you could be shot, become pregnant at a young age, go to jail for drug crimes or any other related crime, or just find yourself in trouble for anything else. I graduated valedictorian even though I would notice major changes in my behavior, mainly my disinterest in school but I did enough to get by.

As for high school, because of the lack of opportunities in my neighborhood I told myself that I would not go to a school there. I wanted different experiences that I didn't think that my community could give me and ultimately that would be the case. One thing to know about me is that I suffer from depression and in retrospect I acknowledge that it probably started when I was in high school.

High school proved to be very difficult for me. I didn't have the same support network that I had, my sister who all my life stayed with my family decided to move with my mom which left me with my brothers. Since they were a lot older than me they never really paid me any attention and I was growing up as well, going through all those hormonal changes learning life lessons about guys and also exploring my sexuality. I would come to realization that I was bisexual and found a community to support it.

Honestly, I don't remember learning much in the classes I took in high school. Although I went to a high school that I felt would have given me more opportunities at success, and believe me it did, I really lost an interest in school. I found that the only classes that interested me were ones that seem to spark my interests. My high school was a vocational school so the program track I was a part of was the business/entrepreneur program. I guess when I think about it now as I wrote that my school didn't teach me to value education it only taught to try to acquire some skills so that I wouldn't be broke, I guess that would predict how I performed in college, but I will elaborate more on that when I get there.

So high school and its highlights are really based on the activities I was involved in outside of school: I was on soccer, did basketball for a small time and cheerleading, was a part of a poetry club and two different programs that were related to dance. One was an afterschool matters program that taught African dance and the other was called "orchesis", or something like that and was taught by a teacher of mine whom I enjoyed very much.

The activities I would really stick to were the debate team and being involved as a student community organizer for a group promoting the well-being of LGBT students in elementary, middle, and high schools. Oh, this makes me remember that I was also president of my school's Gay-Straight Alliance club. I guess it became a blur because all of my LGBT activism work I pretty much group together. I loved my involvement on debate and the community work that I did because I felt it taught me things that I could use outside the classroom and exposed me to chances I would have never gotten by just going to school and coming back home.

Also through my business program I participated in business plan competitions as well which would develop me professionally. I wish I could say I liked high school for the education that I got from it, but I don't feel like I learned much, I made it through high school by my involvement in activities that the school offered. I could get by despite all of the issues going on with my family at the time.

One big change that would happen to me that would impact how I felt about school was my grandmother dying my sophomore year. I never knew what hospice was or what it felt like to watch someone die every day from a disease like cancer, but there it was. I missed my grandmother terribly because my dad worked a lot and my mom had very much so not been in the picture for most of my life and if she was it was like I supported her more than she supporting me.

I got a job first at burger king, got fired after a week, then at a popcorn shop where I worked at least 30-hours a week while going to school and being involved. A year and half later I would be fired and would survive on unemployment benefits through my senior year. I guess I never cared much about high school, because I felt it never changed my material conditions. I was still hungry some days, poor, and on the days where I couldn't afford to get to school I would walk miles from my house to school. Yea, that was high school or at least most of what I come remember of it.

A road less traveled

With all of the things and of ways of not thinking about school, I learned at the high school I attended, of course when it came time to think about college it was a last-minute decision. I did not stack up against the competition and from what I can remember at the beginning of my senior year my GPA was 2.0 or something like that, my ass was barely making it.

I applied to over 20 schools and got accepted into three. What made me decide to go to college honestly being on the debate team did. I never thought about my future or how politics and institutions could affect me until I joined the debate team. I would end up doing really good in high school debate. I would consistently break past preliminary rounds and at one point my debate partner and I became conference champions. What this success meant was getting breaks at meeting attorneys at top law firms in Chicago.

After getting to see what the career field I wanted to be in looked like, I finally realized I had to get a bit more serious about this college thing and put a plan in place to get a better education, because regardless of how I felt about the education I received, going back to my neighborhood without doing anything and not accomplishing anything was not an option. So debate honestly changed my life but also made me realize my intellectual potential

Unmasking the anger

The ignorance and racism here has been one of my biggest challenges. I never knew what the words passive aggressive or micro aggressions meant until I got to this university. White people here look at me like I am something exotic and treat me like I am something to be scared of. If they are not scared of me, they think that they are more superior than me because of the material things that they have.

Trying to not harm a muthafucka here is a daily challenge. I have gotten angrier at the ignorance here to the point where I just feel like I want to lose control and start slapping, hitting, beating those who have the audacity to judge me without even knowing me. At the same time, I am expressing this sort of visceral anger, because mostly I am hurt. I am hurt that even in this age, in an age where I am told by dominant society that bad blood between races should be over and done with, but I still have to go through bullshit. Now I don't think that all white people are evil or anything like that. However, I have just lost all patience for people who chose to engage in this ignorance and think when they encounter me that it is ok.

Black women on this campus I believe are perceived as hostile, ghetto, ill mannered, over sexualized and just dumb. I notice a many time in classrooms since I am a sociology major, where my peers just say some of the most ignorant things about black people and their expectations about black women. When people meet me, I have to put on what I call my "white voice," by making my voice more high pitched so that I don't intimidate the white women that encounter me.

When around white men I feel more of pressure to stand my ground and prove that I am not what they think and smarter than what they think. When people think about ass shaking or exotic dancing they think black women. More than often my ass is the subject of my conversation with white women and how I can dance so well and move it always is an interest of theirs, like I have some magical secret that they are trying to discover.

If I am not any of the things that I speak to above then because of my hair I am exotic. White people ask can they touch it, how does it do what it does, and a plethora of dumb ass questions. I am more than often the teacher of black culture to white people, their cultural tour guide to the black woman experience.

Reflective narrative, Toni

Toni slipped the following handwritten note into my purse while I was teaching during a lecture with undergraduate pre-service teachers. Toni was not enrolled in the class. Her sudden presence surprised me and the students seated at their desk. She entered the classroom quickly and exited swiftly. Toni indicated that the note was a cry for help. She was experiencing a serious mood swing.

> Sometimes I wonder why I am still here/I feel that I have been in every possible situation to flunk out of this university/yet my black ass is still here/I feel like for the next coming year it would be easier to just play dumb/I feel after I am met with so much resistance from students and staff members that it's no point/I can't believe that these many people trust in higher education that have no fucking sense/believe this many people who are close-minded/ on top of me having to deal with bullshit from this institution/I'm over everybody's homepages/and shit but/you know I guess it's because I'm waiting on the black community to do some shit it doesn't know how to do/uplift people who don't always fit the mold of the people/but I digress, I can only focus on those who are here/working to uplift me and I will continue with all of my heart to try to uplift others/I just don't want to kill myself doing it/

The note, Toni

Final researcher's note on Toni: Immediately after class, I called and located Toni. I strongly suggested that she make an emergency appointment with counseling services. She informed me that "they ain't going to do shit!" I convinced her to go anyway. Toni began individual and group counseling. She continues to struggle with depression and anxiety. I continue to be her mentor/muse/confidant/big sister/other-mother. Below is a reflective poem she once shared with me followed by her ethnographic reflections.

5/26/13 – May 26th, 2013

God
I want to know
Who you are
Where you are
Where my mom is
Where my niece is

I want to know where I will end up being

Am I doing everything that I can to make a difference here?

What is my purpose?

I guess I'm trying to agree or find something

I'll never find

~~~~~~~~~~~~

"Your mother is dead." Those are the words my daddy left to me on voicemail as I sat in my African American studies class. I had so much in store for myself that year. I was working so hard. I had been going to counseling for my depression. I had found Audre Lorde and Patricia Hill Collins, finally. It took my fucking junior year, the end of my sophomore really. Up until that time, that I could start feeling that I could be the kind of student I truly wanted to be in undergrad. I could be successful. But then there was the voicemail. And then the missed calls.

There were the text messages that I didn't know how to make meaning of because I didn't know what the fuck was going on. What do you mean she died? How? And what the fuck happened? Where was Phil? He was supposed to be taking care of her and how could his dumb ass let this shit happen. I think I went to the bathroom. I do remember Tierra being there when I told Dr. Powell. She was going through so much herself and helped me. So I cried initially in Dr. Powell's office and then knowing university procedure I immediately went to the Dean of Students Office.

I knew this because this is where I worked for the past two and a half, three years. I worked day in and day out as a student worker, counseling and telling other students of how to do this process when they lost a loved one. "Yes, we can send out a bereavement notification on your behalf." "You have five days according to the university to miss." And the rest of so many other words that I compassionately complied together to tell other about how to piece their life back together after loss. I remember not getting the opportunity to talk to John. My favorite Dean in the Dean of Students office.

I had to talk to David, he was still a cool black guy, but one of those I believe in hard-work and etc. around white people, but then talked about loving his blackness around the black students. He could also be a bit cold, like that black uncle that never wanted to show emotion. But he helped me. David would have given me the money to get home and made sure financial aid would have come through with anything I needed that day. Somehow, in the midst of all, I called my cousin, Tyeisha, now working for Google, helped me so much. She, like me, grew up on the Westside in a fucked up family and was here in the academy then once out grinding to make the life she wanted. She always came through financially. And she gave me more than enough money I needed to get home to make sense of all of the chaos.

From what I could remember I did everything I needed to do on my checklist, talked to the deans and got money to go home. Now back to my apartment I go. I don't remember much of how I got there, but I know it was still messy. I had just been moved after fighting with my passive-aggressive, fake ass, bourgeois black girl roommate. Which my mom lovingly and messily nicknamed the "Flour Girl", because I would tell my mom about the times after she attempted to portray her black self, by frying chicken, and she would leave flour everywhere.

Later that night a reporter called me and asked me did the family have a comment. I don't remember what news station he was from or how the fuck he got my number. I would find out and try to make sense of the death of my mom and niece through news reports, because they knew more than what my family knew. My mom and niece were found unconscious at the scene of an apartment on the Southside of Chicago. They were rushed to the hospital where efforts of life were attempted and failed. Nobody knows how the fire started, but assumed that there were no fire detectors were in the apartment and that there was a possibility that my niece may have started it. I hate that they always say that shit about black kids. You tell me, how does a five-year-old going on six, know how to use a fucking lighter.

~~~~~~~~~~~~~~~~~~~~

6/3/13 – June 3rd, 2013

Some days are easier and some days are harder

Sometimes it hurts you're gone

I never thought that it would be so soon that I would lose you

I admit a lot of days were difficult for us

We wouldn't find solace in each other until later in life, but we would find it, and I would help you just as much as you would help me

I'm not sure how this lawsuit will play out whether or not it's worth it

It doesn't bring you back

~~~~~~~~~~~~~~~~~~~~

Everything in the years to follow were always focused on how to hold back my tears and to make depression look like cold or flu that I came down with. Something that could escape from the body with enough time and effort. I have work to finish and incompletes that came every other fucking semester and sometimes and I just let that shit turn into F's. What could I do, what did they want me to do?

I was depressed and I was grieving, but given the fact that I took 12 credit hours that summer and about 15 to 16 that fall semester everyone assumed that this black girl was fine. Black women are always perceived to be fine in their struggle and fight in this life, because hey, that's what black people, but more specifically black women do, but I was hurting and I was heavy. Not heavy like body fat, but heavy. My body weighed a ton every day when I got up to go and class and then at the end of it all I laid the ton of bricks back to rest just to try to rebuild them back again into something reasonable for the day.

With every award and certificate, I cried for you. And when I failed, I only blamed myself and not you. I was supposed to be able to perform in school because that was the responsibility that I had. At least that's something that my white mentors asked.

"Toni, we know you are smart, but you just don't do the work?" All of these assholes had to have had a meeting about me and decided that they would ask the depressed, grieving black girl why she couldn't perform and would be shocked that her GPA looked like shit because, you know, she was still supposed to PERFORM. And with the help of my mentors of color I did.

I owe everything to Dr. V and Dr. Lorene for carrying me, for pulling me, for helping me to feel like I could walk upright and most importantly that I was capable regardless of the doubts that filled my head about whether I would graduate from this university. When I doubted I couldn't go to grad school and wanted to just work after graduation they looked and me and told me that they didn't give a damn about what my GPA looked like.

That they had sat on committees with folks whose numbers looked like mine or worse and know that those folks still were sitting in someone's grad school. So I did, I looked all over for a place that still had an application deadline open and in all the mental and emotional strength that I could muster I finished one application to the Critical Ethnic Studies program at DePaul University. I remember Dr. Lisa Torres-Meen telling me to write my personal statement from my epistemological standpoint and to let them know what kind of student they were getting. And on May 5th, 2015 I would read these words:

Dear Toni,

I am writing to congratulate you on your admission to the MA in Critical Ethnic Studies program for the fall 2015 quarter. Your official admission decision and welcome package will arrive soon via regular postal service.

My eyes immediately swelled up with tears and I knew that I belonged in the place that other people kept questioning. I cried for you on this day, because I always wanted to open this kind of letter with you. I knew that on that day a week before graduation that you had heard my cries and decided that I could use some good news.

FIELDNOTE 9

AN INCONVENIENT TRUTH

In 2014, I was contacted by Dr. Joyce King who wanted to seek my interest in working with a group of youth organizers in New York. The name of the organization was Girls for Gender Equity (GGE). The organization was committed to programs and advocacy work that serve the needs of girls of color. According to Dr. King, the youth organizers of GGE were in the final stages of an action research project. Participants of Sisters in Strength (SIS) had already collected data on students' and school administrators' perceptions on school discipline policies.

Using radical Black feminism as a framework, the youth participants held focus groups, conducted phone and in-person interviews, and reviewed public records to expose harsh discipline policies in their schools that were directly pushing girls out of school psychologically or physically. The young women's data revealed that girls of color are equally impacted by zero tolerance policies in schools that contribute to the school-to-prison pipeline.

After the first phase (personal observations) of the study, the second phase of the study involved the youth researchers collecting data more formally (interviews, focus groups, surveys etc.) and systematically.

Then, in the third phase of the research project, using methods of action research, the youth researchers decidedly utilized the collected data to inform other girls, the school community, and local political leaders about the harsh realities girls faced in schools. For example, the youth through their engagement with data were educated on sexual harassment in schools, street harassment, harsh discipline policies in schools, and the mistreatment of LGBT youth, and they organized in solidarity with other social justice campaigns like Say Her Name and Black Lives Matter against police violence.

In the spirit of radical Black feminism and action research, research was used in efforts to collectively change their schools and communities according to the youth's interests and needs. Finally, I entered the scene at a time when the youth researchers and their adult counterparts in the organization were interested in introducing their research to the academic community. The introduction of their work in the academic arena might help make their research appear more valid to stakeholders.

Academic researchers are formally trained to systematically collect and analyze data in a supposedly objective manner. Similarly, university researchers follow certain sets of protocols and rules that serve to legitimate the research process and its potential outcomes. Furthermore, like any messages of social justice (i.e. putting an end to harsh discipline policies aimed at girls in schools), one important strategy is to reach wider audiences. The message especially wants to circulate to those who can make a difference as it relates to bringing public attention to the problem, influence policy formation, and providing much needed resources (e.g. financial, technology, land, human, etc.) to help eradicate the problem. In many ways, academic researchers can be an asset to communities.

Conversely, communities can be an asset to academic researchers. Community actors can validate and legitimate our work, and academic researchers can validate and legitimate community efforts—if done in the right way, it does not have to be a hierarchal relationship, but one of mutual understanding, solidarity, and responsibility. Admittedly, it was in the final phase of this action research project with the young women that I came to contemplate my role as a researcher.

I was introduced to the youth organizers and their study, at a time when I had decided to give up on researching my people. I had come to believe that much of education research was exploitative and mostly served the needs of the researcher. As a consumer of education research, I learned that the purpose of most research was to discover how to increase test scores, change student behaviors, or deliver curricular more efficiently or effectively. In juxtaposition, as a university professor, I watched as many graduate students and tenure track faculty scrambled to capitalize on research opportunities that might lead to publication.

We talked for years in conference sessions and (paid) keynote addresses about our research subjects, environments where the study took place, the education problem and our proposed solutions, based on our "research findings." If we were lucky, our research questions, literature reviews, theoretical frameworks, observations, and proposed solutions were published in journals and book chapters. In the meantime, while we were climbing up the proverbial career ladder and moving into middle-class university communities, our research subjects were left behind stuck in the ghettos and barrios, attending underfunded schools or working long hours receiving low wages in dehumanizing work environments. Even worst, at the time that I was being invited to collaborate with the youth researchers, I had adopted the frame of mind that research texts were voyeuristic, intellectual masturbation that found pleasure in poverty, racial, and sexual oppression.

Consequently, I had determined that I would no longer conduct research *on* my people or publish research for the sake of research itself, in a veritable effort to disengage from institutionalized voyeurism and exploitation disguised as "research." Nonetheless, after learning of the mission of the organization, the youth participants' local activism, and finally reviewing their preliminary data, I did not hesitate to join their action research team. Conversely, the organization had become of aware of my line of research and activist pursuits related to organizing against state sanctioned violence, exposing race and gender inequity in schools, and advocating for gender specific and culturally relevant teaching for girls in the U.S. and abroad.

The collaboration was grounded not only in mutual interests (i.e. girls' schooling), but also our partnership was situated in shared responsibility (i.e. analyzing and disseminating data for transformative purposes). Specifically, my role on the research team was to teach the young women researchers *how to* analyze the data gathered and *how to* present their data to an academic audience. In brief, I focused on what it meant to "write academically" and "present academically." Youth researchers were introduced to the rigor of a scientific report—how to write an introduction, conduct a review of the literature and write it up, analyze qualitative data (read: coding and themes), order statistics (e.g. charts and tables), highlight interviewee responses (e.g. direct quotes), and write a conclusion session (i.e. summary and implications for future research).

As one can imagine, the girls were disenchanted with the academic research process. It was boring. They were bored; I was bored. Somehow, I conveyed to the young women researchers that (1) the researcher is detached from the research process, and (2) research presentations are aesthetically reflective of someone else's inclinations and habits of mind. As a researcher, I took on a macro and meso (i.e. community level) view of state sanctioned violence. I knew the statistics and could empathize with the young women's experiences in schools, but I was emotionally detached at that point from education research.

As a mother and activist, I came to believe that education research does not change material conditions nor does it change education practice or policy. Stated differently, I was tired of the *Black girl fetish* in education research, and I refused to participate in the *romanticism and exoticism* of Black girls' and women's bodies and experiences.

In the meantime …

I arrived at the airport looking forward to relaxation time alone on the plane, alcoholic spirits, and the warmth of the sun in Haiti. I had an article submitted for publication and I was ready to celebrate this accomplishment. I waited in the airport security line patiently, because I arrived at the airport two hours earlier than departure time. I thought to myself, "Why are White people always in such a rush and impatient?" I scratched my scalp which was covered by a black headscarf. I knew I looked like a Muslim woman to the White onlookers, when I wore the headscarf.

But, I only wore the headscarf because it was 5 o'clock in the morning, and I did not want to mess up my hair so early in the morning. Also, I wanted to protect it from the dry air and germs on the airplane. Yes, I could have removed the headscarf, but I truly liked being a burden to TSA. A Black woman has never been a threat to this country's security, so they wasted their time, when they asked, "Do you mind removing your scarf?"

Anyhow, I proceeded through security with the other passengers who looked like they had better things to do than stand in line. I wish I had the privilege of acting agitated. I waited patiently showing no emotions. I did not want to appear like a threat to national security. It would only prolong my security check. Finally, it was my turn to meet the sitting TSA agent. "ID and boarding pass." I handed him my passport and boarding pass.

He looked up from the passport, looked me directly in the face, and then looked back down. He passed the passport under a light, then scribbled something on my boarding pass, and handed me back my items. I smirked. In a mild-mannered tone, he replied, "Enjoy your trip. Next!"

Finally, it was my turn to grab a basket. I loaded my carry-on suitcase onto the black conveyer belt, removed my shoes and belt and placed everything into a basket—slid it down the conveyer, and placed the makeup bag carrying all my liquid items into another basket on the conveyer belt.

Then, I carefully walked over to the metal detector "thing" for a scan of my body. Suddenly I heard, "No rings, bracelets, belts. Take everything out of your pocket." I stepped back, removed my huge door-knocker-sized earrings, and dropped them into a small blue basket and proceeded to the metal detector. I was motioned into the machine. I faced the agent, spread my legs apart, turned to the right, placed my feet size 6 foot onto the size 9 footprint stickers on the floor and raised my arms.

I was in the "hands up, don't shoot" pose. Who the fuck was I surrendering too? Does this machine cause cancer? Can the TSA agents on the other side of the screen see my body parts? I hope they can see my big fat ass. What a fuckin' spectacle for their own viewing pleasure. I exited the metal detector.

The male TSA agent put his right hand up in a gesture that meant "stop" or "wait right here." He looked over at a White female TSA agent and she immediately came over to me.

"Do you mind stepping over here?"

In my head, "Yes, bitch, I do mind." "No" came out of my mouth instead.

"Are you wearing any metal, a belt, underwire bra, or are there any keys in your pocket?"

Now, I am irritated. "No."

"Well, I need to do a screening. Are you okay with doing it here or would you prefer a private screening?"

"Here is fine." Just make a spectacle of my body right here in the open.

"Hold out your hands." She rubbed my hands with something on a white cloth, but I was too busy staring at her blue (latex?) medical gloves. Is she contagious or am I contagious?

"Do you mind removing your scarf?"

"No." I knew that question was coming.

Looking at an image on a screen, the TSA agent turns to me and says, "I need to pat down your hair. Is it okay if I touch your head?"

You never touch a Black woman's hair. Total sign of disrespect. My locs are sacred. A reflection of my ancestor's struggle.

"Yes." Clearly, she waited her whole life to touch my crown.

"I'm going to have to pat you down on your breast, back, buttocks, and inner thighs."

She first ran her hands across then under my breast. Next, she rubbed her hand down my back quickly but firmly. She raised my arms and slid her hands down both my sides, from the armpit to my hips. By the time she reached my inner thighs, my muscles were already tense. I clenched my teeth and fixed my eyes straight forward.

On the outside, I was frozen like a corpse, but on the inside my brain was racing. Was I being treated like a prisoner suspected of carrying contraband? Or, was I being treated like a potential terrorist who posed a threat to national security? Or, was I being treated like a slave who was a flight risk? My response: A Black woman has never posed a threat to this country's national security. Therefore, *my existence and will to actively live* is an act of terrorism.

"You're free to go. Thank you." Thank you, but not sorry.

Humiliated, I grabbed my scarf and walked over to my belongings on the conveyer belt. I tucked my scarf into my purse. Other passengers were visibly irritated. It appeared that my luggage and other items were in their way. Now, I was in their way as I grabbed my belongings off the conveyer belt, and I leaned forward to put on my shoes. My dangerous body was an inconvenience.

Shared inconvenient truths in inquiry

Waiting on my flight's arrival to the gate, I reflected on why I was so irritated by the whole screening process, and especially being patted down by the White woman. As a practitioner of mindfulness, I examined my thoughts and emotions (i.e. anxiety and controlled anger) during the episode. It occurred to me that as a sexual abuse survivor, I felt violated by the visual screening of my body and the physical screening of my body. Once again, I was reminded that someone else could have the power to take possession of my body. And, once again, I was forced to detach from my body while pretending to be in control. In my mind, the visual screening was no less invasive as the physical touch. In both cases, strangers claimed access to my body with *coerced* permission.

Second, I have been a victim of police harassment and intimidation in the recent past as a demonstrator against state sanctioned violence, and while growing up in the city as a younger person. For me, the TSA agents were state actors with the power to harass and intimidate me into compliance. State actors represent and enforce racism and White supremacy by determining who will be "pulled over" and "patted down" for the safety of the police and community. The airport in my mind engaged in justified racial profiling with the intent to protect other passengers and the nation. In the airport, I am a suspected terrorist or drug trafficker.

Thirdly, as a mother and aging woman I was at a stage in my life when I was experiencing body insecurities. That morning I went out of my way to cover my curves and ass in order to avoid the "gaze." However, during the security screening, the White gaze was all over me; my hair, ass, and even my emotional expressions were under the watch of the White other. Ironically, in that moment I was unclothed, touched, examined, probed, and fondled publicly.

After a long wait, the agent at the gate scanned my boarding pass, and said, "Thank you for flying with …" I was still in a fog as I allowed myself to acknowledge my feelings. I headed toward my assigned seat. Once I found my assigned seat letter and number, I sat down, and began to people watch. People are irritated with other passengers who take too long to find an open space in the overhead luggage compartment. I am glad that I learned early to pack light and carry a smaller luggage piece. I did not want to inconvenience the other passengers or bring any unnecessary attention to myself. Once everyone was settled, I looked out the window seat and smiled.

I smiled because at that moment on the plane, the following thought popped into my mind: this is how those Black girls feel every day. They feel violated! As the young women researchers explained in their research reports, at school they are required to walk through metal detectors, and school safety officers frequently request that they remove hair accessories to check their hair for foreign objects; and the girls are randomly screened or patted down, and demanded by school safety officers and other school officials to have their belongings checked.

Similar to my arrival at the airport, the young women also arrive at school with their unique set of experiences.

For the young women, they were being "screened" as they coped with issues associated with the adolescence stage of development. Adolescent school girls are more body conscious and they are more likely to be concerned with how others perceive them, especially their peers. Thus, to bring attention to the young women during the screening process could cause anxiety or anger. Furthermore, many of the young women researchers and their school-age peers were survivors of family, neighborhood, and state violence. The metal detectors, screenings, and unwanted touch and attention only further violated them and could potentially be triggers that could lead to anxiety, anger, and depression.

In closing, in the same manner that my dignity (if not civil rights) was taken away from me that day in the airport, the young women's dignity is violated at schools daily. Based on self-reflection, reflection on the girls' life experiences inside and outside of schools, conversations with the young women, and the collected research data, I came to realize that state sanctioned violence does occur in schools in highly gendered ways.

With this epiphany, the challenge for me as a researcher was to help the girls convey their experiences and emotions throughout the research process. How do we bring our research to life in a way that audiences can feel what we feel as we walk this world as young/Black/woman/researcher/participant? We need data analysis techniques that are reflective of youth culture and Black girlhood (or Black womanhood), and analysis processes that are an embodiment of our lived experiences across cultural contexts. I hope daughtering as an analytic tool demonstrates these multiple perspectives and embodiments.

FIELDNOTE 10

TEXT MESSAGE

A call and response

Apr 10, 2014, 2:26 PM

VENUS:

Hi Skyye. It's Dr V. Is there a time on a Tues or Thurs that you can have a late lunch or early dinner?

SKYYE:

Thursday I believe is best for me ma'am. Like 6:30

VENUS:

Girl, that's dinner! I was thinking between 3:30 and 5pm.

Apr 15, 2014, 2:45 PM

VENUS:

I'm available today and Thursday.

SKYYE:

Today is not good. Thursday

And thank you.

And question…

Why do you sound so serious in these txt? Or am I reading into it too much?

VENUS:

Do I sound serious? I guess I need to work on my text talk lol

SKYYE:

Uuhhhhh, yes. For my age group things like "Lol" and "jk" etc. are like a life and death situations in a txt. FOR REAL. Gotta make the words come alive

Thursday. And thank you once again. Take Care Doctor.

Or else the receiver may let their imagination take it the wrong way. But hey, just wanted to make sure I didn't offend you. ☺ But alright... see you Thursday

Apr 17, 2014, 11:08 AM

SKYYE:

Doctor Winters what time today?
If we're still going

VENUS:

3:30 works for you?

SKYYE:

That's good

VENUS:

Cool

SKYYE:

Where to?

VENUS:

My office 3:30

Apr 17, 2014, 1:54 PM

SKYYE:

? Where is your office?
And are we eating at your office? Cause if so then I'm not going to dress up as I had originally planned.

VENUS:

DEG 355 not eating in office

April 23, 2014, 11:00 AM

SKYYE:

Doctor...Hey, do you at all buy black art?

May 1, 2014, 1:29 PM

SKYYE:

I was saying "forgive me" for end portion of that test. ☹
You'll see what I mean.
Well, anyways it was great having you Doc! See you!

VENUS:

Haha! Thank you!

Jun 6, 2014, 12:06 AM

SKYYE:

Up thinking about my mama

Some reason you crossed my mind.

Up?

Jun 6, 2014, 11:23 AM

VENUS:

Ha! No, I go to sleep early, and wake up early.

How are you feeling now?

SKYYE:

Better

I txt my daddy

I have my nights

VENUS:

That will happen for the rest of your life. Great, you're normal!

SKYYE:

Sweet molasses It's like I could hear your voice as I read that last txt. Lol And mmhhm, sometimes. But thank you for the words though. Or should I say Care Mrs Winters or should I say

diagnosis….? Oo Doctor… And oh yea, I'm currently reading Copper Sun. I like it so far. Read it? Probably so. I'll talk to you one day about it.

Jun 6, 2014, 2:18 PM

VENUS:

Dr Winters or Dr V. I hate Mrs.—archaic

SKYYE:

Don't know what that means

But okay Doc

Yes'm

VENUS:

For me, I don't like my whole identity tied to my marital status. I've accomplished a lot beyond marriage. Ms. is fine. Doc better ☺

Jun 6, 2014, 8:58 PM

SKYYE:

> Okay

Jun 18, 2014, 7:20 PM

VENUS:

> If there is one or 2 Black women in history who you would most identify with, who would it be?

Jun 18, 2014, 9:02 PM

VENUS:

> Couldn't tell you ma'am. I hardly know any honestly. And the ones I do, I don't know much about.
> Sorry.

VENUS:

> Informative.

SKYYE:

> Not good though.

Jun 20, 2014, 10:04 AM

VENUS:

> What is a hobby of yours? Or how do you relax?
> I'm asking these questions because I'm trying to get a portrait of who you are as a student and as a person.

SKYYE:

> I love to read. Had my piano thing going on for a while. Still has my keyboard. So that too ... Our praise dance ministry at church Sewing is relaxing to me too. I'm not heavy in it, but if something small needs to mended I do so Hanging with good friends Hanging with my daddy You're fine.

VENUS:

> Do you keep a diary or a journal?

SKYYE:

> Prayer journal

VENUS:

Nice. Do you mind sharing a few entries with me? You can take a pic(s) and I'll try to read it.

SKYYE:

Girl whatchu tryna do? Get a new case study for one of your books?! Hold on.

VENUS:

Yes lol

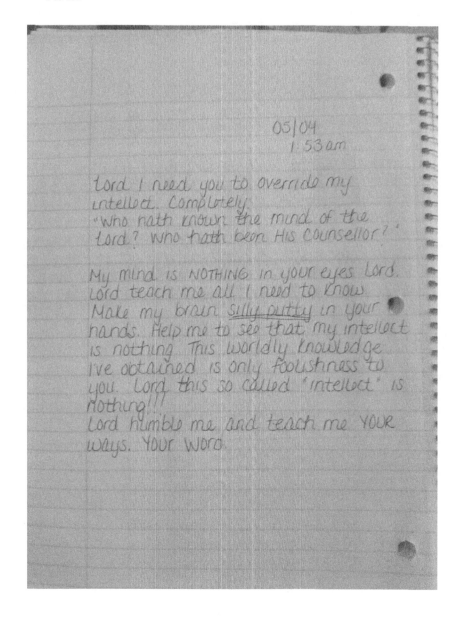

05/04
1:53 am

Lord I need you to override my intellect. Completely.
"Who hath known the mind of the Lord? who hath been His counsellor?"

My mind is NOTHING in your eyes Lord. Lord teach me all I need to know Make my brain silly putty in your hands. Help me to see that my intellect is nothing This worldly knowledge I've obtained is only foolishness to you. Lord this so called "intellect" is nothing!!!
Lord humble me and teach me YOUR ways. Your Word.

SKYYE:

That heavy stuff I gotta keep personal.

SKYYE:

Light.

VENUS:

Real good

VENUS:

It's deep.

SKYYE:

And that quote came from Romans 11:34

Just didn't write it

Stop tryna butter me up. You'll get more maybe. Sheesh.

VENUS:

Lmbo!

SKYYE:

Naw, but thank you.

To God be the glory

Smh.

Doctor…

Lol

VENUS:

That's deep! For real! You just taught me something ;-)

SKYYE:

Thank you

VENUS:

Welcome

SKYYE:

That all you be needin Masta? Greens on the stove.

VENUS:

Yes, unless you want to volunteer one more ☺

SKYYE:

Alright doc! ☺

SKYYE:

Thoughts centered on the Shummanite woman whose son died.

VENUS:

What made you relate to this situation? Or this scripture?

SKYYE:

Can't really remember… Back in December. But I think I was dealing with doubt and fear. Problems with trusting God and always tryna fix things for myself instead of letting him.

No wait

Family problems. I think that's what was going on. My feelings

December 18
'13
11:49 pm

Just as the woman who's son had died her response in all the chaos remained "It shall be well, It is well." Her circumstance did not dictate her mood or faith level in God.

~~Just like her faith - her~~

Just like her response: . Her faith remained constant. God is moved only by faith. When everything around her began to shift and alter, her faith didn't.

The most devastating thing that could of happened did happen: Death of a child, but rather than losing her mind she ran to the man of God.

God is looking for us to run to Him in calamity.. Not lose our minds!

When we have faith in God's power, He'll show us His power!

VENUS:

Oh ok. So this was a reminder that you can rely on God even in the most difficult of times. Get it.

SKYYE:

Yes. Exactly. Chaos, Calamity and or Craziness …my God still sits on the throne. It's my faith in Him that has kept me and will keep me. At the end of the day: "It is Well."

Don't get me preaching doc! Lol

VENUS:

You have so much faith to be so young. It's to be admired. One more question. I promise. 😐

SKYYE:

To God be the glory.

Go head

VENUS:

How does your faith sustain you through schooling, education, college, etc.?

SKYYE:

It's knowing that there is nothing out there in the world that could ever measure up to living for God. Nor anything more important than it. He comes first. At school and as far as education I trust God to "get me the grade". Yea I work hard, but I don't lose my mind over assignments, projects or tryna be the straight A student. I feel sorry for those types of people. Cause I know it's temporary! A degree is good, but that degree can't love me, it can't remind me of who allowed me to go to school in the first place. God would never bless us with an opportunity/something just so we can fail in it. If God placed you there then He's going to give you every tool you need to do well. ⋆unless you decide to mess it up⋆ Ya know? My confidence is not in professors or the curriculum… It's in God. It's Him that allows me to do well, not really me.

It can't breathe life into me in the morning, it can't speak to me, it can't take away misery and it definitely can't get me into the kingdom. It was and is God

School is good.

But it's not everything.

VENUS:

You have an old soul. That's a compliment.

SKYYE:

I hear that a lot

Nickname was granny back in HS

in a good way. Lol

VENUS:

Mine too! For real! Crazy….

SKYYE:

But thank you

And Ana Mae

How were you back in HS?

VENUS:

Like I am now. Lol Very astute, meaning into learning. Respected adults but talked too much. Impulsive and made bad decisions at times. Always kinda did what I wanted to do and say what I wanted to say.

SKYYE:

A fire…

To you

VENUS:

Yup. But, I went through a lot as a kid. I was coping back then. For ex, I never turned down a fight lol

SKYYE:

Lol, had a niece like that.

Did you like always defend yourself type of thing-personality?

VENUS:

Yup. Always had to prove that I was not going to let nobody bully me. I used to start fights with bullies. Middle child syndrome I guess.

SKYYE:

Funny cause I was actually the one who was bullied in HS. Freshman year that is. Passive.

VENUS:

Well, ain't it good to know that I would've protected you 😎

SKYYE:

Girl please.

VENUS:

Don't beg lol

I hated bullies. But maybe because my younger sister was quiet and passive too. I took on all her battles.

SKYYE:

Gone somewhere. Lol

You know the type of voice I typed that in. Lol.

That was a smart mouth comment! Not the other one!

Y'all close?

VENUS:

We need a Black English translator with sounds.

Yes, we are really close.

SKYYE:

That's good.

I think if my mama had had another child we would be.

VENUS:

Are you close with your girl cousins?

SKYYE:

Yes. Cousin that became my partner in crime in HS. Same age. Monica.

And an older cousin who's in her 30s. Lives in Georgia.

VENUS:

What Monica up to now? Just curious.

SKYYE:

Wife, mother, in school

I've found that many of my cousins and girlfriends my age got "left behind."

SKYYE:

Really? Left behind how exactly?

She is doing well. Just a lot on her plate.

VENUS:

Usually early pregnancy and raising children trumped going away to college. Of course some, if not most, continued going to school with a child. But, it definitely slowed them down and we ended up taking different paths in life.

SKYYE:

It does. But what can you do? It happens. It's an obstacle, but not defeat. But it wasn't just her. Me and a lot of my old friends are on different paths. Not necessarily for those reasons though. Life.

Yeah. They only make us stronger and more committed to education for self, family, and community. That's what's up.

It's funny because back in HS me and my boyfriend at the time had planned to get married in college. Lol. Young & Dumb. If we hadn't broke up I think me and my cousin D would've been in the same boat.

But honestly I feel like the path she took worked for her.

For me... I think it would've been disastrous. Her life situation was vastly different.

VENUS:

As I always say, with my friends, family members and sister, there is no right path. Some paths are more difficult for some individuals while other paths are easier for some.

SKYYE:

Do you consider yourself on your path already or still getting there?

VENUS:

Chile, whew...good question.

I'm on the path that I chose. It was the path for me based on who I was at a particular time in my life. At times, I question my courage. Why didn't I take a different path? Did I take the easy way out?

I'm proud of women who took the road less traveled. This—college—grad school, etc.,–was the easy way out. But, now, I feel like I'm in the belly of the beast.

I stay because the lifestyle is easy, and I stay because I meet women like yourself. We need each other. But, I now these institutions can be very oppressive.

Spirit kill

SKYYE:

Doctor Winters I think you did the best you did with what you had. And like I don't know....... like sometimes............... Wait, how cool are we? I'm not about to say something to hurt you, but something I noticed. Not tryna overthrow your elder-ship over me.

And I'm sure you've noticed a lot about me too. Actually, I'm sure of it.

Can we get semi deep for a moment?

If not it's okay. Really. Not just saying that.

VENUS:

Yeah, let's get deep lol

SKYYE:

Doc...

Like… you seem so angry to me. I be thinking: does she hate and like
people at the same time?

Ya know? I don't know…

Or did I overthink?

Lord please take it the wrong way….

By the way this is a back and forth thing… so you can do the same for me.
Get me?

Just being open

VENUS:

No, you didn't overthink. I have been very angry over the last 6 months or so.
In fact, I just read something I wrote back in March and I thought, damn I
must've been angry lol

Skyye, racism is so prevalent in education and many are getting away with it. I'm
angry because Black folks don't challenge it, and White folks are gloating in it.

I feel bamboozled because I thought education, or at least educated folk,
were different. They can be even worse, because they hold true power.

SKYYE:

But you don't have to be angry. And the thing about it,. people are always
gonna bamboozle and act power hungry. Smart, dumb, rich, white, black etc.
It's gonna be that way til the end of time. But don't let that nonsense dictate your mood or how you feel about life and what not

Doctor some folks are literally raised to be that way. You know that.

You can't change that!

And yea racism is a huge bother. I feel it too. But don't stay angry….

And not all whites are gloating.

It's gonna bring about your ruin doctor Winters. You can't keep harboring
all these feelings. Our bodies aren't designed for that. Sickness comes from
that. But you know that already.

I LOVE YOU DOCTOR WINTERS!

☺

VENUS:

Lol Don't try to butter me up now 😒

:/

I hate seeing people broken.

Hurt.

Lol!

I do love you!

VENUS:

Um hmm (lips twisted)

SKYYE:

It was in no way by coincidence that you and I met and became fairly
acquainted.

I think of you and I pay attention.

In class and on Facebook

You don't believe me?! Lmbo

VENUS:

Yeah, fortunately, I never stay angry. The benefits/curse of coming from a big supportive family. Also, my service work in Ghana is a spiritual retreat that fills me up. It's healing work.

It's okay to be angry, especially if you signed up for the fight; however, one can't be consumed by it. One has to move on at some point. I do. You see my anger, but as we get closer, you will recognize it as rage and passion.

I'm only angry from 12:35–1:50pm lol

SKYYE:

Rage is not good! Passion is!

Ghana causes the anger to leave?

Dude.

That time slot better not be for EAF.

Lol

VENUS:

Hahaha

Rage can be good as well: a violent desire or passion.

Ardor; fervor; enthusiasm: poetic rage.

Black women are dying from keeping our anger bottled up inside. Dying of cancer and hypertension and diabetes. That's actual research findings :-/

SKYYE:

I'll dictionary it. Lol

I believe it.

Which is why I'm an advocate for counseling and partook in it myself for like a year.

VENUS:

Were you once angry? Or for something else? And, yes, Ghana takes me away from White supremacy and capitalism, while bringing me closer to nature, godliness, and myself.

SKYYE:

Oh yes! Lotta craziness after my mama died. Whew! I began to have weekly counseling sessions with a Pastor. I cried so much the first day that my face was still the same even the next day. I went to school and my friend was like... ... uhhh. Lmbo

This was in college though.

When in Champaign

VENUS:

What finally made you decide to go to counseling?

SKYYE:

Broke down at a church service and like one of the mothers got the Pastor to come talk to me. Thereafter he asked like when and if I was available for talking. Few days later I'm there. I couldn't bear it anymore. All that "what happens in this family stays in this family; stuff had to go!

Even til this day we keep in touch like bi weekly just because.

I couldn't even explain the joy and peace I had after I started going.

VENUS:

I agree. Counseling works. I wish more Black women participated in it. We are the mules of the Earth. Yet, we don't talk about our pain, anger, depression, and resentment, due to trying to save face and protect our own.

SKYYE:

Zora Hurst Nelson? That it? But yea. I was like forget that. I'm getting healed from this! I'm glad I went through it though. It made me sensitive to stuff like that. Especially for youth.

But it's a lot of walls to get past.

One of my babies actually revealed last week that she was molested when younger. Never told anyone. Still so young. I want her to talk... she kinda has. And I feel like one of my little kings was too. Ima wait and see though.

Know a book for these type of things?

VENUS:

Black Pain, Can I Get A Witness, How Long Does it Hurt

SKYYE:

Thank you

VENUS:

The first 2 are more for Black women and issues of depression, etc. The last one is for teens surviving sexual abuse

SKYYE:

Thank you

And one last thing Doctor Winters.......

VENUS:

You're welcome. And yes?

SKYYE:

LOVE YOU! :-D *even though you may just be using me temporarily for one of your writings or something, experiment etc. but I don't care!* Lmbo. Lite rally! Have a grand day today! Good talking to you! ☺

VENUS:

Love you back! No experiment. You're stuck with my mean passionate enraged self ☺

Jul 9, 2014, 10:56 AM

SKYYE:

Doctor....

I have somebody that wants to meet you....

eye roll

Don't get conceited now.

Jul 9, 2014, 3:18 PM

VENUS:

Too late. Been dat. 😓
When you in town?

SKYYE:

I'll let her know and then y'all can go from there

VENUS:

Cool

Feb 10, 2016, 2:28 PM

SKYYE:

Doctor.
Hey lady.
How are you?

Feb 18, 2016 11:58 AM

VENUS:

Hey! Girl! How are you? How's teaching? Married life? So good to hear from you. Been thinking about our great conversations.

Feb 18, 2016, 1:30 PM

SKYYE:

I'm good! Married life is good! We're in the process of moving. I know you weren't aware, but I did send you an invitation via Facebook. Did you see it?

But yes, me and mister are good. I'm out of college, married and loving life right now. Also I'm fully in the ministry now. I preach every few months at my church along with the other ministers. No babies yet though.

And yea I thought about the text we used to send, and I was like "I wonder how she's doing?"

Sat, Feb 25, 2017 2:39 PM

VENUS:

Hey, Ms. Skyye. How's the family, baby, and you? ~DrV

SKYYE:

> Oh my hey lady! Been so long! We're all doing well!
>
> Little mama turned two months this week and me and hubby are doing well. Full time mommy and wife now. Life is good! How about you and the crew?

Fade to black.

FIELDNOTE 11

DE-CODING THE COVENANT

Daughtering as methodology

Daughter [daw-ter]

noun

1. A female child in relation to her parents.
2. Any female descendant.
3. A person related as if by the ties binding daughter to parent.
4. Anything personified as female and considered with respect to its origin.
5. Chemistry, physics. An isotope formed by radioactive decay of another isotope.

adjective

1. Biology. Pertaining to a cell or other structure arising from division or replication.

Rituals

1. Read, listen to, or watch a piece of "data" (or slice of culture). Take about 15 minutes in a well-lit room to think about what the data might represent and how it relates to a current social or political issue. Think about what the data's relationship is to a cultural group and particular social context.
2. Before the sun sets, approximately 7pm or 8pm, depending on time of the year, take a long walk or run. Two to four miles is ideal to get the blood flowing and wake up the muscles. The point of this exercise is to become with nature and to begin to connect receptors in your brain. Music is okay; the beats and rhythms may be stimulating for the heartbeat and mind. See and hear the birds, feel the wind, chill, or sun. Contemplate your data on this run.
3. At home, cool down with a fresh glass of water. Replenish the body. Grab a writing journal and just write.

4. Right before bed time, sit at the ancestor altar. Acknowledge each ancestor individually. Thank them for what gifts and traits they have passed on to you. Be sure to smile. Be in conversation. Ask your ancestors for guidance, strength, tenacity, resilience, and wisdom. And, the gift of creativity. Sit with your ancestors quietly for approximately 15 minutes.

5. Before closing your eyes to sleep, welcome the ancestors to visit you in the night and give them permission to give you insight and clarity on your research questions or issues. Be sure to place water near your bedside. You may also want to sit an ancestor's image somewhere in plain sight. Be prepared to have a restless night. Many ideas and images may come in throughout the night until early morning.

6. First thing in the morning at 4:30am, before even rising, thank your ancestor(s) for the wisdom. Sit quietly in a reflective state for approximately 20 minutes. Listen to the birds. Watch the sky. Be mindful of your breathing. Contemplate how messages received in the night connect to your data considerations.

7. After 20 minutes, practice early morning yoga (20–30 minutes) and deep breathing meditation (15–20 minutes) for approximately 45 minutes. During meditation, state your intentions for the day. Does it include writing? Does it include reading? Does it include creative practices like drawing, sewing, painting, dancing, etc.?

8. After the above exercise, visit the ancestor altar for the morning and just sit with the ancestors. Light a white (or your ancestor's favorite color) candle to open up the space and your mind.

9. After breakfast (e.g. toast, peanut butter, banana, and grapefruit—a plant based and chlorophyll filled diet is best when doing contemplative work), set aside at least 20 minutes to write something related to your data. Contemplate interpretations of data and best methods for representing such data that would be meaningful and respectful to all implicated by the data.

10. Clean the air with sage or burn an incense (e.g. frankincense) that inspires positive energy. Sit near a window with bright sunlight. Analyze and write.

Black women and other feminist and womanist scholars have already established the worth and legacy of mother scholars and sister scholars; but we have under-theorized the act of being a Black daughter. Daughtering is a worldview that shapes your state of mind, and it is a way of being and navigating the social world. Daughtering teaches us how to love those whom may have harmed us, and loathe those who have harmed those we love.

At the same time, daughtering necessitates us to respect and seek to understand *how* "the extraordinary, the magical, the wonderful, and even the strange come out of the ordinary and the familiar" (Thiongo, 2008, p. 758). Daughtering comes with no instructional manual or moral handbook. We learn to be daughters through deliberate but keen observation, and at times, direct command. At other times, we drop to our knees or altars to ask for guidance on how to be better daughters to mama or grandmama, or to mother Earth or Afrika, or god(dess) herself.

As daughters, we learn early to serve. Serve the men folk, serve the young, serve the elderly, serve the mother. As daughters, we are taught to think critically. "Nobody gone think for you." "Stop acting dumb." "Use common sense." "Act like you got some sense." "You den' lose your mind". "Actin'like you ain't got the sense you was born with." Daughtering demands that you think for yourself, and speak up for yourself and other people's daughters.

Because mothers tell us the stories and our mothers are the original keepers of the secrets, sometimes we forget in our methodologies of telling that women were daughters before we were women. Daughtering like mothering/other mothering informs our worldview (methodologies, inquiry, data analysis, etc.). Daughtering does not require the use of words like epistemology and methodology—we only use them when we have to (prove ourselves to outsiders). We learned to use such words after our mothers sent us off to faraway lands and placed our heads into the hands of other people—foreign people—who used big words, sometimes unnecessary words.

Daughtering implores us to decode such words and tolerate the pain of other people's interpretations of our tresses, bodies, language, behaviors, dispositions, personalities (or spirits?), and figure out how the foreigners', our new caretakers, words/constructs collided with or meshed with everything our mothers taught us about being faithful and obedient daughters.

Daughtering demands that we try to understand that the foreigners did not always align with the images of them that we saw on television. On television, they were always happy and rich, welcoming and smart with a basic vocabulary. Up close and in person, the White foreigner disappointed many of us and fell short of the ideal student or omnipotent all-knowing professor.

Daughtering as a "student" required us to be tolerated or patronized for the sake of science. Or, to become "cultured." Fortunately, daughtering is not passive. In fact, it is quite subversive, watchful, and clandestine for the sake of survival. We are socialized to read in between the lines. The foreigner (descendants of the colonizer) never learned or accepted that the Black daughter is quite knowledgeable—she is the knower, yet, always mistaken for the known. She is power. Daughtering, as methodology, invokes her power; epistemologically mothers/other mothers/mothering informs these powers. Sitting on front porches, back porches, at the kitchen tables (or sinks), or on a living room floor "getting our head did," we were initiated into the cult of Black daughterhood/womanhood even when unbeknownst to us.

Daughtering as a process or identity is not necessarily genetic, but spiritual, and the spiritual affects the physical, behavioral, corporeal, and cerebral. Daughtering reminds you that you are never alone in the world. You are always somebody's daughter, sister, niece, cousin, or spiritual descendant. Kinship requires responsibility. Imagine that every piece of data analyzed implores a daughter scholar to think about how her interpretations and representations would affect her living and deceased relatives near and far.

Every time we re-member (Dillard, 2012) or share stories of our past(s), we know that we are potentially invoking our ancestors' memories. Daughtering requires us to be mindful of the memories we share orally or in writing for every time we speak, we may be inviting ancestors in to not so sacred spaces. Recently, I have heard young daughter scholars refer to "non-sacred" spaces as unsafe spaces (e.g. college classrooms, academic conferences, faculty meetings, etc.). Our daughters are advised not to share when space does not feel safe, when doing memory work, but many of us will engage in memory work to make a space feel safer, familiar, or help us be braver in the face of the unfamiliar.

The purpose of education was not to take us away from our families or communities for that matter. The purpose of education was to give us access to other forms of knowledge that our parents or local resources and networks (e.g. churches, libraries, religious texts, etc.) could not provide. The purpose of education was to help us bring forth ... alternative and additional resources, skills, knowledge, and wisdom to our respective families and communities. Knowledge of the self also brought forth the necessary wisdom needed to transcend the confines of race and gender (and any other worldly identities that shifted across contexts) that means little or nothing after we left this Earth (for the ancestral world).

Daughtering invites an imagining of the possibilities of knowledge. How does engagement with inquiry and data serve my family, my communities, my self-worth, and the person I want to become? How might knowledge of science help me become more humane, the world a safer and comfortable place, and help me understand the purpose of my life? What does a slice of culture, text, artifact represent to my daughter, someone else's daughter, or a mother of a daughter or son? How can I help my analysis relate to the lived experience of a daughter? An ethics of daughtering? Daughtering embodies an ethics of love (hooks, 2000); emotionality is not taken into consideration in institutional research protocol protections, in essence, it is forbidden.

As an ethic of love, daughtering conjures creative expression. Daughters' data representations might be shared through dance, a poem, a piece of prose or a song; or perhaps it would present itself as a hair pattern adorned on top of a girl's or woman's head—or present via a sharp tongue or an act of refusal. In scientific thought, daughtering looks like questioning, resisting, and deconstructing universal truth claims, grand narratives, and essentialism, while simultaneously, walking in and exposing our own contradictions. Daughtering obliges that we embrace our multiplicity and seek to express our data representations as multivocular and multi-textual.

As daughters, we were taught how to observe the unseen, contemplate the ignored, interpret the forgotten, and analyze the taken for granted, and speak the forbidden. In our knowledge pursuits, we make it a point to be transdisciplinary for: We watched our mothers become sociologists on front porches, economists at the dining room table, chemists in the kitchen, psychologists in other women's living rooms, political scientists every election cycle, and historians interpreting and passing down family history, women's history, African and African American history.

Black daughters learn early how to navigate multiple terrains of history and consciousness. Consequently, as daughters, our tools of analysis for the de/construction and manipulation/interpretation of social reality will inherently, and conscientiously, require transdisciplinarity. Our experiences as daughters entail migrations across borders, geographies, neighborhoods, social groups, languages, and dialects. For example, by the age of nine, I lived in nine different locations. Daughtering necessitates one to be in tow, or mobile, never permanent, but fluid and flexible or adaptable.

Daughtering as a disposition reminds us in the data analysis process that identity, location, words, ideas and even disposition itself, even when recorded as text, are never static or permanent, but malleable and flexible, depending on context and time, and one's "location" in life. Further, the ability to comprehend the nature of adaptation (read: shape shift) and the vulnerability of transient people, daughtering acknowledges and centers resilience in the analysis process. How has the person's life been molded by social circumstance (as a daughter, sister, cousin, niece, partner, citizen within a certain geopolitical context) beyond her control? In what ways has vulnerability been forced upon her, and she been implored to show tenacity? How has her strength developed her into a resource for her community and society? Or, how does a sheet of music, song lyric, dance move, or poem represent the vulnerability and agency, adaptability of an individual or group of people? The daughter as an interpreter of data bears witness to the vulnerability and agency of *the least of these brothers and sisters of mine.*

As daughters, we have come to believe that the purpose of knowledge pursuits is to identify and bring forth our individual (and collective) talents and abilities. We presuppose that the research process can be potentially oppressive for both the researcher and researched; therefore, we conscientiously strive to interrupt its hegemonic past and choose to draw upon it as a vehicle for liberation. Daughtering insists that we always strive to contemplate how the inquiry process and data interpretations can disrupt spirit murder. Data and data performances can be spirit—energy.

Daughtering permits us daughters to consider that one piece of data could have multiple interpretations and meanings and we give meaning to that data based on our positionality in the social world. We also avert that our knowledge claims are not in competition with other daughters, but we assert is unequivocally in opposition to colonial, neocolonial, and White supremacist scientific pursuits and propositions. Schooling is akin to spirit murder (Wing, 1997, p. 28) for many young women of color; therefore, the quest for knowledge should be a rekindling of the spirit.

As our kinfolk fight against alienation and isolation at home, Black feminist data analysis processes must serve to synchronously armor and humanize Black people. In closing, our data approaches are improvisations that at times purposively blur the boundaries between fact/truth and fiction/drama. Daughtering puts forth our approaches to science (fiction). The poetics of daughtering are our mosaicism. Because our very existence as Black women unfold in a series of stages and beseeches collective wisdom and resourcefulness, Black feminism/womanism in qualitative inquiry materializes as mosaic.

REFERENCES

Akbar, N. (1998). *Know thyself.* Tallahassee, FL: Mind Productions and Associates.

Angrosino, M. V., & Mays de Pérez, K. A. (2000). Rethinking observation: From method to context. *Handbook of Qualitative Research,* 2, 673–702.

Carruthers, J. H. (1999). *Intellectual warfare.* Chicago, IL: Third World Press.

Collins, P. H. (1998). *Fighting words: Black women and the search for justice.* Minneapolis, MN: University of Minnesota Press.

Collins, P. H. (2004). *Black sexual politics: African Americans, gender, and the new racism.* New York: Routledge.

Collins, P. H. (2000). Gender, black feminism, and black political economy. *The Annals of the American Academy of Political and Social Science,* 568(1), 41–53.

Collins, P. H. (2002). *Black feminist thought: Knowledge, consciousness, and the politics of empowerment.* New York: Routledge.

Davis, A. (1993). Black feminist thought: Knowledge, consciousness and the politics of empowerment. *Teaching Philosophy,* 16(4), 351–353.

Davis, A. Y. (2011). *Women, race, & class.* New York: Vintage.

Denzin, N. K., & Lincoln, Y. S. (2000). (Eds). Introduction: The discipline and practice of qualitative research. In *Handbook of qualitative research* (pp. 1–2). Thousand Oaks, CA: Sage.

Dillard, C. B. (2000). The substance of things hoped for, the evidence of things not seen: Examining an endarkened feminist epistemology in educational research and leadership. *International Journal of Qualitative Studies in Education,* 13(6), 661–681.

Dillard, C. (2012). *Learning to remember the things we've learned to forgot: Endarkened feminism, spirituality, and the sacred nature of research and teaching.* New York: Peter Lang.

Evans-Winters, V. E. (2005). *Teaching black girls: Resiliency in urban classrooms.* New York: Peter Lang.

Evans-Winters, V. E. (2017). Necropolitics and education. In *Between the world and the urban classroom* (pp. 19–33). Boston, MA: Sense Publishers.

Evans-Winters, V. E., & Esposito, J. (2010). Other people's daughters: Critical race feminism and Black girls' education. *Educational Foundations,* 24, 11–24.

Evans-Winters, V. E. & Love, B. (Ed.). (2015). *Black feminism in education: Black women speak back, up, and out.* New York: Peter Lang.

Giddings, P. J. (2014). *When and where I enter.* New York: HarperCollins.

Guy-Sheftall, B. (1995). *Words of fire: An anthology of African-American feminist thought.* New York: The New Press.

hooks, b. (2000). *Feminist theory: From margin to center.* Cambridge, MA: Pluto Press.

King, J. (2005). *Black education: A transformative research and action agenda for the new century.* New York: Routledge.

Ladson-Billings, G. (2000). Racialized discourses and ethnic epistemologies. *Handbook of Qualitative Research, 2,* 257–277.

Ladson-Billings, G., & Tate, W. F. (1995). Toward a critical race theory of education. *Teachers College Record,* 97(1), 47–68.

Lee, C. (2005). The state of knowledge about the education of African Americans. In J. King (Ed.), *Black education: A transformative research and action agenda for the new century* (pp. 45–72). New York: Routledge

Lynn, M., & Dixson, A. D. (2013). *Handbook of critical race theory in education.* New York: Routledge.

McClaurin, I. (Ed.). (2001). *Black feminist anthropology: Theory, politics, praxis, and poetics.* New Jersey: Rutgers University Press.

Mullings, L. (1997). *On our own terms. Race, class, and gender in the lives of African American women.* New York: Routledge.

Payne, C. M. (1984). *Getting what we ask for: The ambiguity of success and failure in urban education.* Westport, CT: Greenwood Press.

Rabaka, R. (2010). *Against epistemic apartheid: WEB Du Bois and the disciplinary decadence of sociology.* Boulder, CO: Lexington Books.

Reagon, B. J. (1993). *We who believe in freedom: Sweet Honey in the Rock—still on the journey* (Vol. 1). New York: Doubleday.

Roberts, D. E. (1997). *Killing the black body: Race, reproduction, and the meaning of liberty.* New York: Pantheon Books.

Souljah, Sister (1994). *No disrespect.* New York: Random House.

Spector-Mersel, G. (2010). Narrative research: Time for a paradigm. *Narrative Inquiry,* 20(1), 204–224.

Taylor, E., Gillborn, D., & Ladson-Billings, G. (2009). *Foundations of critical race theory in education.* New York: Routledge.

Thiongo, N. W. (2008). *Wizard of the crow.* New York: Knopf Double Day.

Walker, A. (1983). Zora Neale Hurston: A cautionary tale and a partisan view. In *In Search of Our Mothers' Gardens: Womanist Prose* (pp. 83–92). San Diego, CA: Harcourt.

Welsing, F. C. (1991). *The Isis papers: The keys to the colors.* Chicago: Third World Press.

Wing, A. K. (Ed.). (1997). *Critical race feminism: A reader.* New York: NYU Press.

INDEX